NOT IN HEAVEN

Contemporary Jewish Thought
from Shalem Press

Essential Essays on Judaism
Eliezer Berkovits

God, Man and History
Eliezer Berkovits

The Documentary Hypothesis
Umberto Cassuto

*The Dawn: Political Teachings
of the Book of Esther*
Yoram Hazony

Moses as Political Leader
Aaron Wildavsky

New Essays on Zionism
David Hazony, Yoram Hazony, Michael Oren, editors

NOT IN HEAVEN

THE NATURE AND FUNCTION
OF JEWISH LAW

ELIEZER BERKOVITS

With a foreword by
Joseph Isaac Lifshitz

SHALEM PRESS
JERUSALEM AND NEW YORK

Third Printing, 2015

First published in 1983 as *Not in Heaven: The Nature and Function of Halackha*

Cover design: Erica Halivni
Cover picture: © RMN/Jean-Gilles Berizzi
Paris, musée d'Art et d'Historie du Judaïsme

Printed in Israel

Distribution:
Shalem Press, 3 Ha'askan Street
Jerusalem 9378010, Israel
Tel.: (02) 560-5577

E-mail: shalemorder@shalem.ac.il
www.shalem.ac.il
ISBN 978-965-7052-55-6

R. Yehoshua rose to his feet and exclaimed:

לא בשמים היא

It is not in heaven.

Baba Metzia 59b

CONTENTS

Foreword

In his study of the Jewish community in Eastern Europe, focusing on the period from the sixteenth century to modernity, Jacob Katz described two authority figures—the rabbi and the *maggid*. The rabbi, the devoted Torah scholar, functioned chiefly as halachic authority. But it was not the rabbi's door that was always open to those in need of advice and inspiration; that was the role of the *maggid*. The *maggid* preached weekly sermons before large audiences, while the rabbi preached only twice a year—on the Sabbath of Penitence preceding the Day of Atonement and on the Great Sabbath preceding Passover. The difference between the rabbi and the *maggid* lay not only in the degree of their interaction with the Jewish masses; they also differed in their intellectual pursuits: the rabbi devoted most of his time to the study of Talmud and Jewish law, while the *maggid* turned his attention to mysticism.

The figures of rabbi and *maggid* can usefully serve as archetypes in investigations of Jewish intellectual and social life in other times and places, too, beyond the scope of Katz's historical study. The rabbi represents a leadership whose authority derives from an intellectual ethos and is bound up with the law as passed down and interpreted in the systematic halachic tradition for generations. Consequently, his influence wielded on the community comes "from above." By contrast, the *maggid* represents a leadership whose authority is charismatic, located "in the people"; that is, he acts from within the community and maintains direct contact with its members. Consequently, his influence comes "from below." The rationalistic world of law and jurisprudence constitutes the rabbi's spiritual environment, while the *maggid*'s world is a poetic or narrative one, abounding with all the sensuous, emotional, and mystical richness of human life.

In the national life of the nascent Jewish people, this paradigm seems to have been embodied in the clear-cut opposition between Moses, teacher of the law, elevated above the people, whose holiness made him remote and inaccessible, and Aaron the priest, lover and pursuer of peace, arbitrator and promoter of brotherly love, who became Moses' spokesman. Several sources attest that a parallel social distinction to that obtaining between the rabbi and the *maggid* existed between agadists and halachists in the talmudic period. For instance, R. Abahu (the agadist) was awarded great honor in Caesarea and lauded as "Great man of your people, leader of your nation" (Sanhedrin 14a), while R. Akiva's colleagues counsel him: "Akiva, what have you to do with agada? Cease your talk, and turn to [the laws concerning defilement through] leprosy signs and tent-covering!" (Hagiga 14a).

A similar dichotomy is evidenced in the Middle Ages. Certain sages, some of them widely acclaimed, were known as preachers (*darshanim*). Their renown stemmed from their righteousness and oratorical skill, in contradistinction to other sages of their time, whose greatness was attributed to their erudition

in Torah and their status as legal authorities. For example, Rabbi
Judah Hehasid was revered as a holy man blessed with divine
inspiration, not necessarily due to his command of Talmud
and Jewish law. In reply to a question from Rabbi Judah, Rabbi
Simha of Speyer explains why it is permitted to drink milk, even
though most animals are ritually unclean after slaughter, and
consequently theirs is the milk of a nonkosher animal: "Well do
I know that you have put me to the test out of your great affec-
tion for me, asking me that question about milk; you should
have asked me about meat, for even when an animal is examined, and its meat pronounced permitted for consumption,
who has given that permission, inasmuch as most of them are
not really kosher..."* Rabbi Simha treats Rabbi Judah Hehasid
with the utmost respect, answering his query as though Rabbi
Judah were testing him, but in fact he dismisses the question
altogether; in rabbinic historian Ephraim Urbach's words: "Here
we have another example of the difference between the legal
authority, who decides what is permitted on the strength of law,
and the pious man, cautious and tending to prohibit, due not to
strength of *law* but to strength of *awe*."**

We may regard the two great Jewish streams in Eastern
Europe—*mitnagdim* and hasidim—in light of the distinction
between these two types of spiritual leaders. The *mitnagdim* can
be considered the intellectual descendants of the rabbi, and the
hasidim are those of the *maggid*. Indeed, several disciples of the

---

* *Shibbolei Haleket* 2, p. 58. *Responsa and Decisions of the Rabbis of Ashkenaz and
France,* in MS Bodl. 692, ed. and notes Efraim Kupfer (Jerusalem: Mekitzei Nir-
damim, 1973), p. 8 [Hebrew].

** E.E. Urbach, *The Tosafists,* p. 413.

Baal Shem Tov (Rabbi Israel of Medzhybizh) were *maggidim*:
Rabbi Dov Baer, the Maggid of Mhezirech, and Rabbi Yehiel
Michel of Zlotchov. The role of the *maggid* greatly influenced
the formation of Hasidism, both in its appeal to the common people and in its spreading of mysticism. By contrast, the
mitnagdim, even when they did pursue Kabbala, did so unob-
trusively, concentrating instead on the study of Talmud and
codes of law.

The division of roles between "rabbi" and "*maggid*" was per-
petuated with the subsequent emergence of the *Musar* (religious
self-improvement) movement. Rabbi Israel Lipkin Salanter rev-
olutionized the Lithuanian yeshivot by demanding emphasis on
moral development alongside study and ritual observance. His
movement, placing as it did man at the center, also continued
the *maggid* tradition with its renowned *maggidim*, such as Rabbi
Jacob Joseph, the Vilner *maggid,* and Rabbi Moses Isaac Dar-
shan, the Kelmer *maggid,* both disciples of Rabbi Salanter. The
musar yeshivot enacted a separation of functions, the head of
the yeshiva being charged with the instruction of Talmud, and
the *mashgiah* (moral supervisor) with fostering a personal relationship with the students; the latter also gave the *musar* talk, a
reincarnation of the maggidic homily. Although these addresses
treated ethical matters for the most part, they were never completely removed from theological issues, in the manner of Rabbi
Haim of Volozhin. An exploration of human nature was the
central theme.

I point out and exemplify the distinction between the rabbi and
the *maggid* because it sheds light on Rabbi Eliezer Berkovits'

philosophical personality. At the Slobodka yeshiva—where Berkovits' thought germinated—pupils studied mainly Talmud, setting aside about half an hour daily for the study of ethical literature. What set the yeshiva apart was its emphasis on human greatness. Rabbi Nathan Tzvi Finkel, known as "the Alter (Elder) of Slobodka," founder of the yeshiva and its spiritual supervisor, placed great emphasis on Adam as the humanistic model. The Alter preferred morality sessions to Talmud lessons, not unlike a community *maggid*. The following is a portrait of Finkel and his thought by his disciple Rabbi Yehiel Jacob Weinberg, later to become director of the rabbinical seminary in Berlin:

> The Alter's strength lay mainly in his insights into human nature in general, and Jewish nature in particular. "We still don't know man, his strength and the achievements of which he is capable": "God created man in his own image"—this biblical verse should not be read in passing: we must seek to grasp it in all its profundity. Concealed beyond the material-external reality we perceive of as the human body and its physical needs is a dynamic-creative spiritual essence with qualities of the great Creator, blessed be his name.

> The Alter reiterated this important idea throughout his life, entrancing his audience with his original formulations, basing his lessons upon biblical verses and dicta of the sages, thereby shedding new light on them. In his talks in his home, in the yeshiva, and on our walks together in the fields, he elaborated at length on his notion of man shut away in his prison, awaiting redemption and revelation—in other words, creation. The power of creation is given to man. Man's Creator gave him this power, of unlimited potency and scope. Man, when he so wills, can reach the heavens.

Who's to stop him? The theory of ethics seeks answers to this question.[*]

This humanistic worldview filtered down to Rabbi Berkovits when he was a student of Rabbi Weinberg's at the rabbinical seminary. A conception of man as the pinnacle of Creation, and morality as a tenet of Jewish law—these are the principles of Jewish thought that he learned from his teacher. Rabbi Berkovits, then, was nurtured in the maggidic tradition. As a disciple of this humanistic strand of the tradition, he entered the University of Berlin. His theological outlook, which he developed while a student at Rabbi Weinberg's yeshiva, stood in opposition to the idea of an alienated God as taught at the university. Rabbi Berkovits found an abstract, transcendental conception of God disturbing, not just when couched in the terms of modern philosophy but also as found in medieval Jewish philosophy. He could not accept an abstract God who does not care for man, his own creation. At the university, Rabbi Berkovits also took issue with Kantian ethics as minimized to the sum total of all obligations deriving from abstract categorical imperatives, an ethical view of the individual and his life as mere objects subordinated to the operation of behavioral rules. Although Rabbi Berkovits drew on his extensive knowledge of philosophy from his university days for the purpose of developing his ideas, his homiletic method and his deepest theological and moral convictions were shaped by the yeshiva, where he was exposed to the perspective that was to form the foundation of

---

[*] Rabbi Yehiel Jacob Weinberg, *Responsa Seridei Esh*, pt. iv, Rabbi Nathan Tzvi Finkel (Jerusalem: Mossad Harav Kook, 1977), p. 310 [Hebrew].

his entire world. The Slobodkan worldview, the leitmotif running through all of his essays, is a moral framework that places man at the center of Creation, with morality being the major aim of halachic life. Clearly, Rabbi Berkovits did not see eye to eye with formalistic Jewish thinkers. The school of halacha in which Rabbi Berkovits' thought developed was one that propounded the principles of morality and justice.

The *musar* movement had many opponents, whose claims were founded mainly on fear of innovation, of changing the tradition. But there was also more substantive philosophical criticism. For instance, one of the movement's vociferous detractors, Rabbi Abraham Isaiah Karelitz, the Hazon Ish, denounced in particular the movement's antinomianism. In his view, halacha is to form moral life; no core of values exists outside of it: "Moral obligations at times coalesce with the rulings of halacha into a single entity, with halacha's determining what is morally prohibited or permitted."* The Hazon Ish did not contest the importance of morality but believed that a solution to moral problems could be found not by perusing ethical works outside of halacha, but rather within halacha itself: "And the essential thing for curing these ills of the soul is the study of halacha as meticulously as possible, until it is ingrained and produces absolute love of the law."** Studying volumes of moral instruction, as adherents of the *musar* movement did, was liable to cause damage worse than that wreaked by those who made no effort to mend their ways:

---

* Rabbi Abraham Isaiah Karelitz, *Hazon Ish: On Faith, Confidence and Other Matters* (Tel Aviv: Ministry of Defence, 1979), p. 21 [Hebrew].

** Ibid., p. 25.

People who possess good qualities and study books of moral behavior when they are young but do not study law, and thus have no love of the law in their hearts—such people are more likely to abuse the law than those who never pored over books of moral behavior, since the evil spirit is wont to cause obstinacy and arrogance in scholars, who then look down on common people, as if the scholar is set high above them, and anything he does appears in his own eyes generous and dutiful. It is but a laughing matter to him whether he is suspect of abusing the law, "for my actions are always on the right side of the law, as moral as could be."*

According to the Hazon Ish, morality falls within the scope of Jewish law; ethics shouldn't be treated separately from it. Moreover, when moral betterment is unrestrained and untempered by knowledge of the law, it may lead to a mistaken and hence immoral decision.

To the Hazon Ish's criticism must be added a no less vexing problem: might not the elevation of the moral life to a higher level than the observance of ritual law be construed as belittling the ultimate objective of observing the commandments—closeness to God? Space does not permit us to reply to these criticisms in full, yet it should be emphasized that Rabbi Berkovits is not calling for an ethics dissociated from halacha. According to him, halacha does not contradict ethics at all when the student of Torah is aware of the moral aspect of the law. Rabbi Berkovits opposes formalistic legalism that ignores the moral underpinnings of halacha. Unlike the Hazon Ish, who advocated pure halachic meticulousness, Rabbi Berkovits

---

* Ibid., p. 27.

proposes *halachic study* geared toward uncovering the intrinsic moral values of halacha.

I shall draw upon a talmudic source affording a glimpse into the ethical thought of Rabbi Berkovits. The Talmud recounts a contest between priests that ended in a murder on the ramp leading to the altar:

> Our rabbis taught: It once happened that two priests were equal as they ran to mount the ramp, and when one of them came first within four cubits of the altar, the other took a knife and thrust it into his heart. R. Tzadok stood on the steps of the Hall and said: Our brethren of the house of Israel, hear ye! Behold it says: If one be found slain in the land... then thy elders and judges shall come forth... On whose behalf shall we offer the heifer whose neck is to be broken, on behalf of the city or on behalf of the Temple Courts? All the people burst out weeping. The father of the young man came and found him still in convulsions. He said: "May he be an atonement for you. My son is still in convulsions, and the knife has not become unclean." [His remark] comes to teach you that the cleanness of their vessels was of greater concern to them even than the shedding of blood.*

The continuation of the talmudic passage explains that the tragedy went beyond the murder itself. The fact that the father, upon discovering that his son has been murdered, is more concerned about the ritual cleanliness of the knife than about his son's death—this is what the rabbis of the Talmud found so

---

* Yoma 23 a, b, Soncino English translation.

heinous. According to them, *that* was the tragedy that caused Rabbi Tzadok to cry out on the steps of the Temple Hall. The juxtaposition of this human incident with the halachic problem clearly indicates the talmudic sages' priorities. Halacha devoid of morality—a life of halacha that has sterilized the moral life—is unacceptable from the halachic perspective itself, and certainly fails to achieve its purpose.

In this volume, Rabbi Berkovits is crying out, as Rabbi Tzadok did on the steps of the Temple Hall. At the core of his many books and essays is a ceaseless striving to reconcile morality with traditional practices. Writing in the terrible aftermath of the Holocaust and its destruction of the Jewish world, Rabbi Berkovits mourned the loss of the world of Torah. Unhappily he witnessed attempts to restore the world of Torah and Jewish law and preserve halachic scholarship after most of the talmudic scholars had been lost, by inclining toward the written text—an orientation that had more than a hint of formalism about it—and a concomitant neglect of man and his moral values. As a modern *maggid*, Berkovits called for a return to the moral life, a return that is not at odds with halacha, but acts within halacha itself.

Joseph Isaac Lifshitz
Jerusalem
Kislev 5770/December 2009

Introduction

The term "halachic Judaism" needs some explanation. It is not to be understood as a form of Judaism that is opposed to agadic Judaism, a distinction propagated by some authors. There is no such thing as agadic Judaism. Halacha and agada are intrinsically interrelated. The great halachists of the Talmud are also the great agadists. I use the term "halachic Judaism" on the basis of my understanding of the meaning and function of halacha. Halacha is the bridge over which the Torah moves from the written word into the living deed. Normally, there is a confrontation between the text, which is set, and life, which is forever in motion. Even such an apparently easily understood commandment as "Thou shalt do no manner of work on the Sabbath day" requires lengthy explanation. There is an obvious need to define what is meant by "work." As soon as one undertakes that task, he is involved in the confrontation between a real-life situation and a text. There are innumerable possibilities for human behavior and action, innumerable human needs and problems arising from them. How to apply to them the specific definition of "work" requires further explanation and interpretation. How to face the confrontation between the text and the actual life situation, how to resolve the problems arising out of this confrontation, is the task of the *Torah sheb'al peh*, the Oral Law. This second Torah, ever since the days of Moses, handed down from generation to generation, accompanies the *Torah shebiktav*, the Written Word, along its journey of realization in the innumerable concrete situations through which the Jewish people passes in the course of its history. It is the wisdom of Torah implementation in the daily life of the Jewish people. It makes the Torah *Torat hayim*, living teaching and relevant law. The essence of the Oral Torah is the halacha. As the root of the word (*haloch*— walk, go) indicates, halacha teaches the way along which the Jew is required to walk in accordance with the Torah. Halacha is the application of the Torah to life. But since there is no such thing as life in general, since it is always a certain form of life at a specific time in history, in a specific situation, Torah application means application to a specific time in a specific situation. The result of this process is what I call halachic Judaism.

Our generation has witnessed probably the most radical transformation of the conditions of Jewish existence since the destruction of the Second Jewish Commonwealth in 69–70 C.E. On the one hand, European Jewry—its many-centuries-old communities, its entire living tradition and its numberless institutions of learning, its experience and wisdom, accumulated through the ages and handed down from generation to generation—an entire national culture and civilization, has been wiped out by international inhumanity and barbarism. On the other, we have been granted the miraculous return of our decimated people to its ancient homeland, as it always not only hoped but knew would one day happen. This greatly weakened people, in the diaspora as well as in the State of Israel, is confronted with unparalleled challenges to Jewish physical as well as spiritual survival. The Torah has to become effective anew in the midst of revolutionary changes in the world as well as in the condition of the Jewish people. There has never been greater need for halacha's creative wisdom in applying the Torah to the daily realities of human existence than in our day. Maybe our generation has to learn that wisdom anew. We certainly have to become aware of it anew. It is essential that halacha regain its original nature and function. As a contribution toward that end, we have undertaken this study as an attempt to define the nature and purpose of classical halacha. On the basis of what we have found, we have also given some indications of the direction in which we believe it is incumbent upon us to move in the present situation.

The interested student, familiar with talmudic learning, will find a treatment of our subject that is much more intensive, both in breadth and in depth, in our work *Halacha: Its Authority and Function*, recently published in Hebrew by Mosad Harav Kook in Jerusalem.

Finally, may I be permitted a personal confession. While all my life I have endeavored to take my stand on the foundations of halachic Judaism as it was handed down to me in my father's house, and as I have acquired it from my studies in yeshivot and later from my great teacher Rabbi Yehiel Weinberg, of blessed memory, at the Hildesheimer Rabbinical Seminary in Berlin, in this work I was determined to be guided exclusively by the traditional halachic material as I found it and as I have learned to understand it over the years. My ideology did not produce this work; the work fortified the ideology.

NOT IN HEAVEN

CHAPTER ONE

The Nature and Function of Jewish Law

The Torah is all-inclusive. It embraces the entire life of the Jewish people. Halacha, therefore, has to interpret the intention of the Torah for all areas of Jewish existence: the spiritual, the ethical, the economic, the social. It also has to define the functions and powers of the teaching and implementing authority envisaged by the Torah. In what follows, I will examine three important ways in which the halacha translates the intention of the Torah into application in the real-life situation: (i) As guided by common sense, or *sevara*; (ii) as the wisdom of the feasible, according to which the law must maintain its applicability in practice; and (iii) as the priority of the ethical, according to which it is understood as furthering the larger moral principles embodied in the Torah. In the concluding section, I will explore in detail the ways in which these principles are put into practice, as shown in the example of marriage and divorce laws.

COMMON SENSE

All interpretation is first of all an activity of the intellect. It is important to note the degree of authority that the Talmud ascribes to logical thinking, to the insights of common sense, which the rabbis refer to as *sevara*. In a number of talmudic passages it is taken for granted that the *sevara* is no less authoritative than the biblical text itself. Often, when one of the rabbis attempts to justify an opinion by basing it on a verse in the Torah, the question follows: "What need is there for a verse? It is a *sevara*—that is, the opinion may be based on reasoning alone.[1] The meaning of the question is: Since the opinion under discussion may be established by common sense, the text used for its validation seems superfluous. But since there can be nothing superfluous in the Torah, the text quoted must be teaching something else.

The principle of the *sevara* is effective in every area of talmudic law. We shall consider several examples. Two rabbis of the Talmud discuss the legal form of acquiring movable property. According to Resh Lakish, one has actually to take possession of the object by pulling it, lifting it from the ground, or causing it to move. He bases his opinion on a verse in the Bible. R. Yohanan, on the other hand, maintains that possession is taken when the purchase money is handed over to the seller. However, he cites no biblical proof for his view. Writing in the fourteenth century, the commentator R. Yosef bar Habiba explained: "R. Yohanan does not derive his opinion from a biblical text. He bases it on *sevara*. For most property is actually acquired by means of money."[2] It is significant, however, that while R. Yohanan has no biblical proof for his view, he considers it sufficient to state that "it is the word of the Torah"—that is, it is by the authority of the Torah that money is the legal means of acquiring movable property.

In another context we learn that if a woman, of whose marital status nothing is known, appears before a court and asserts that she had been married but is now divorced, she is believed; she may remarry without providing any further proof that she is divorced. The ruling is based on the principle that "the mouth that bound her [as a married woman] is also the mouth that releases her [by also stating that she is now divorced]." One of the rabbis in the Talmud, R. Asi, attempts to justify the principle by pointing to a verse in the Bible that supports it. This justification, however, is rejected, for "what need is there for a biblical proof? It is a *sevara*—the same mouth that bound her also releases her."[3] If you trust her statement that she was married, you also have to trust her statement that she was divorced. The principle is applied in numerous other areas.

The authority of the *sevara* emerges clearly from two other examples. Since the commandments of the Torah were given to us that we may live by them, the rule is that if a Jew is forced to violate any commandment under threat to his life, he should transgress rather than die. However, there are three exceptions to the rule. They are idolatry, sexual prohibitions such as adultery and incest, and murder. One must accept death rather than commit any of these three sins. Whereas the rule in the first two cases is derived from the Torah, in the case of murder one relies on a *sevara*. It is told that once a person came to Rabba and told him that the ruler of the city had ordered him to kill someone; if he disobeyed, he himself would be killed. What was he supposed to do? Rabba answered him succinctly: "What makes you think your blood is redder than that of your fellow man?" Maimonides offers the following interpretation: Reason tells us that one may not destroy a life in order to save another. It is remarkable, therefore, that this rule in the case of sexual prohibitions is derived from the rule concerning murder; according to talmudic understanding, the Bible compares the seriousness of a sexual attack on a married woman to that of an attack upon the life of a person. Just as one should die rather than commit murder, so should one refuse to violate the sexual laws, even under threat to one's life.[4] The Talmud bases the ruling in one case on a comparison to the ruling in another—but to one that is nowhere mentioned in any biblical text and whose authority is assumed to be known on the strength of its reasonableness.

In another case, the power of the *sevara* is affirmed even more boldly. According to biblical law, if a woman remarries after a divorce, and the second husband then divorces her or dies, she may not return to her first husband. The Talmud discusses the question of whether this law applies only when the marriage to the second husband had been consummated or even when the woman was only formally betrothed to him.[5] The majority view holds that even if only the legal betrothal had taken place, the woman, once divorced from her second husband, may not remarry the first.

This view, however, presents us with a hermeneutical problem. The biblical text tells us the reason for the prohibition of remarriage to her first husband: "Since she had been defiled."[6] How does this apply to a woman who was only engaged to another man but did not live with him? The rabbis explain that this reason applies only to the case of an adulteress, whose husband is barred from remarrying her. This, of course, contradicts the plain meaning of the text. The Bible speaks in general terms that apply to every case in which a divorced woman remarries and after a second marriage wishes to return to her first husband. To limit the ruling to the case of an adulteress renders the text unintelligible. Moreover, we have a rule that in no interpretation may the plain meaning of the text be disregarded. One of the most authoritative commentaries on the Talmud, that of the Tosafot, explains that in this case, the plain meaning of the verse was suppressed because it did not seem to be right to say that a woman who married another man was "defiled" by that marriage. Her second marriage was legal and completely moral.[7] Only an adulteress may be described in such language. In this case, on the strength of a *sevara*, a new meaning was forced upon the biblical text, violating its simple meaning.

Occasionally, even a new law that departs from a prevailing rule may be created by a *sevara*. According to a well-established principle, the Torah frees a person from responsibility for the results of external compulsion, any "act of God," any normally unexpected event or unforeseen circumstance (*ones rahmana patrei*). Nevertheless, Rava, one of the great talmudic authorities, declared that this rule does not apply to cases of divorce: If, for instance, a man hands his wife a writ of divorce on condition that the divorce will take effect only if a certain event takes place, he cannot later deny the divorce by arguing that the event took place unexpectedly, against his will, outside the normal course of possibility. In other words, a woman who would have remained married according to the generally recognized biblical rule, since the conditions of her divorce would have not been considered fulfilled, is judged to be a divorced woman, free to marry again, according to the new ruling of Rava.

How may this exception to the rule be justified? Rava ruled on the basis of his own *sevara*. He was saying: Let us consider the likely consequences of the general rule. Assume that a man gave his wife a writ of divorce with the explicit condition that the divorce would take effect only if he did not return from an upcoming trip to a foreign country within twelve months. If he then does not return, there are two possibilities: Either he does not wish to return, in which case the divorce is effective; or he does wish to return but because of some "act of God" is prevented from returning, in which case, in accordance with the general rule, the writ is not valid and his wife is not divorced. Assuming that there is no possibility of communication between the husband and wife, what might be the consequences in such a situation? The more conscientious woman will in most cases assume that if her husband has not returned at the end of the given period, he is probably unable to return due to circumstances beyond his control. She will consider herself still married and possibly remain an *aguna* for the rest of her life.[8] Another woman, less conscientious in matters of marital fidelity, will readily be inclined to believe that her husband has not returned because he does not wish to; therefore, the condition of the divorce has been met, and she is a divorced woman, free to look for another mate. Both, of course, may be wrong. In actual practice such a situation would be intolerable. Therefore, the general rule governing external compulsion cannot function in the area of divorce. If a divorce is given conditionally, the husband and wife are to be informed that once the condition is fulfilled, no matter for what reason, the divorce becomes valid.[9]

We have seen, then, that:

(i)   Principles deriving from a *sevara*, from common sense or logic, have the validity of a biblical statement;

(ii) The Torah itself makes reference to a ruling by a *sevara*, assumes it to be known, and by comparison to it establishes its own ruling in a case in which the *sevara* on its own would not have been able to give the biblically required decision;

(iii) A *sevara* may be so convincing that it may compel one's conscience to suppress the plain meaning of a biblical injunction and force upon a verse in the Bible a meaning that it can hardly bear textually;

(iv) A *sevara* may show that in certain areas the consequences of a generally prevailing law would be unacceptable and, therefore, that those cases must be exempted from the authority of that law.

The importance of the *sevara* also throws light on another aspect of halachic legislation. In case of disagreement between rabbinical opinions in the Talmud, the rule is, in accordance with the biblical verse, to follow the majority opinion. Yet on numerous occasions this principle was not followed; the opinion of an individual was accepted against that of the rest of his colleagues.[10] In most of these cases, no reason is given for the deviation from this biblically based rule, but occasionally one may derive from the talmudic discussion what it was that guided the teachers of halacha in this matter. R. Yose maintains that one may not grant power of attorney to another person by sending him word via a messenger. The majority of the rabbis disagreed with him. Yet Shmuel taught that the halacha was according to

R. Yose. When the son of R. Yehuda Hanasi remonstrated with him about this, Shmuel answered him: "Be quiet, my son, be quiet. Had you known R. Yose personally, you would realize that he always had his reason for his opinion."[11] In another case, R. Elazar, the son of R. Shimon, disagreed with the view of his colleagues. One of the rabbis ruled that the halacha was not according to R. Elazar. The Talmud asks: "That is obvious! [There is no need for saying so, since the rule is that] when an individual goes against the many, the halacha is according to the majority." The Talmud answers that in this case, it was necessary to state explicitly that the rule was not according to the minority, because otherwise one might determine that the minority opinion was correctly reasoned, and, therefore, one would have to decide against the majority; it was stated in order to prevent that mistake.[12] In the case of R. Yose, we accept the minority opinion because it is more convincing than that of the majority; in that of R. Elazar, one has to warn against the minority opinion because the reasoning behind it might be seen as convincing. Other examples of this nature appear in the Talmud. On one occasion an opinion of Shmuel is contradicted by an authoritative earlier source. The verdict presented on Shmuel's view is *tyuvta*, which normally means defeat in talmudic discussions. But despite this, the halacha follows the teaching of Shmuel, because his reasoning is sound.[13] Sound reasoning overrules an authoritative text.

Thus we have gained an insight into the functioning of the majority rule. That an opinion is held by the majority of scholars is no proof that it is true. A majority may be no less mistaken than a minority. Therefore, follow the opinion that is based on logically valid reasoning. If the *sevara* of the minority, even if it be a minority comprising a single person, is convincing, accept it. When there is no reason to prefer the minority view to that of the majority, when logically the two are equally compelling, only then follow the majority. The majority rule is not a logical principle but a pragmatic one. Thus, the rabbis were able to say that the minority opinions have been preserved in the talmudic sources, and not just those of the majority, so that if a rabbinical court at a later time should for some reason of its own agree with the minority, it would have the right to invalidate a previous ruling according to the majority. And it could do so even if the first ruling was handed down by a rabbinical court greater in learning as well as in number than was the second.[14]

THE WISDOM OF THE FEASIBLE

Especially since the time of Immanuel Kant, a distinction has been made between two kinds of reason. One is theoretical, dealing with the categories of logical reasoning; the other is "practical," and its subject matter is the laws of ethical reasoning. Correspondingly, in halacha, theoretical reason found its application in the "Thirteen Rules" in midrashic and talmudic literature that the rabbis used in interpreting the biblical text. A comprehensive study of the Thirteen Rules would give us a treatise on talmudic logic. Our concern, however, is chiefly with the "practical" reason of halacha. We use the term in a twofold sense: Halacha facing the practical needs of human existence, and halacha teaching the application of ethical principles in the midst of the daily life of the Jewish people.

That the Torah was not given to the ministering angels of the Almighty is self-evident. A number of halachic rulings were based on this insight. But if so, the Torah must pay attention to human nature, to the human condition, to human needs. That this is indeed so, the rabbis found confirmed in an important biblical injunction.

In order to humanize the conduct of soldiers engaged in a war, the Jews were commanded:

> When you go forth to battle against your enemies, and the Eternal your God delivers them into your hands, and you carry them away captive, and see among the captives a woman of goodly form, and you have a desire for her, and would take her to you for a wife, then you shall bring her home to your house; and she shall shave her head, and pare her nails, and she shall remove the raiment of her captivity from off her, and shall remain in your house, and mourn her father and her mother a full month; and after that you may go unto her, and be her husband, and she shall be your wife.[15]

Considering the barbarous behavior toward women in conquered territories in time of war prevailing even in our own day, this law of the Bible was revolutionary. According to rabbinic interpretation, one could take a captive woman only for a wife, and one had to treat her as a wife. Notwithstanding its ethically innovative nature, the rabbis of the Talmud thought that the law needed further justification. The Bible obviously condemned the lawlessness and cruelty with which conquered people, and especially women, were treated by victorious armies. Why did it not forbid the taking of captured women against their will altogether? The explanation given is that this law was given with a view to the "evil inclination" (*yetzer hara*), which is part of human nature.[16] In light of the force of the sexual instinct in man, in the prevailing conditions it would have been useless to command its complete suppression. By ordering the soldier who desired a female captive to take her for a wife, the Torah was educating people toward humane behavior, toward an understanding of the injustice done to the captive woman.

This interpretation reflects the talmudic understanding that the Torah does not command anything that man, because of his intrinsic nature or the prevailing conditions, would not be able to do. This realization is the basis of a ramified series of halachot. According to the Torah, one must not marry the divorced wife or the widow of a brother. But if a man dies without offspring, it is a biblical commandment for his brother to marry the widow, so that through the building of a new family the name of the deceased brother may be preserved. This is known as *yibum*, or levirate marriage. If, however, the brother refuses to marry the widow, the ceremony of *halitza* is necessary, by which the woman is freed to marry whomever she pleases. According to this rule, the levirate marriage takes precedence over the *halitza* separation.

Nevertheless, during the mishnaic period, the rabbis reversed the order, arguing that *halitza* is preferred.[17] What was the reason for this? The explanation given is as follows: As a rule, a man must not marry the former wife of his brother; an exception, however, was made in the case of a brother who died without leaving children. In such a case, one fulfills a divine commandment by marrying the widow, in order to raise a family that will be considered as if it were that of the deceased brother. However, it was found that most people who would marry the widow would not do so for the sake of the *mitzva*, in order to preserve the name of a brother. People usually marry for personal reasons, because of attraction or other personal interests. Given human nature as the rabbis knew it, the biblical commandment was not realizable. Therefore, according to some commentaries, the levirate marriage was forbidden; according to others, it was only discouraged. According to the one, a biblical law was abolished; according to the other, it was greatly reduced in meaning and importance.

To understand this, it is important to recall a talmudic principle: "Where it is possible, it is possible; where it is not possible, it is not possible."[18] Let us look at some of the examples given. Assume an elderly or sick man lives away from his wife in a "land across the sea," a faraway country without the possibility of communication. He might be a man without children. If he should die, his wife will not be free to remarry whomever she wants, for the man has a brother, who may want to fulfill the commandment of the levirate marriage, or else will have to release her through the *halitza* ceremony. The husband wishes to relieve his wife from such dependence on a brother; therefore he sends her a writ of divorce. It takes some time before the messenger arrives. In the meantime the husband dies because of illness or old age. In such a case, the divorce ought to be invalid, for a divorce cannot take place after the husband's death. Nevertheless, the Mishna states that the messenger should hand the woman the writ under the assumption that the husband is still alive. This accords with the halachic principle of *hazaka*, or presumption, according to which a condition, once established, is legally assumed to continue unchanged until the opposite has become known.

In another authoritative source, however, it is taught that if a *kohen*, a member of the priestly caste, gives a writ of divorce to his wife on the condition that it will take effect just before his death, his wife must immediately refrain from eating food that is *teruma* (the share that was given to a priest from the yield of the land). In this case, the wife is of Israelite parentage; as long as she is married to a priest, she may benefit from *teruma* on account of her husband. But once she is divorced, she returns to her Israelite status; like any other Israelite, she is barred from deriving any benefit from the priests' share. In this case, as soon as she receives the writ of divorce, even though it becomes valid only immediately prior to her husband's death, she is already considered an Israelite woman. This is due to the possibility that her husband may die at any moment, in which case she would already be divorced now.

The two sources seem to contradict one another. In the case of the divorce document sent from a faraway country, the husband is presumed alive as long as we do not receive information to the contrary; in the case of a woman married to a *kohen*, we do not make that assumption, and instead take into consideration the possibility of his death. In attempting to resolve the contradiction, the Talmud offers: "You are comparing *teruma* to divorce? *Teruma* is possible; divorce is impossible."[19] The meaning is: For the woman married to a priest, it is relatively easy to make arrangements to live on food that does not have the sanctity of *teruma*. But the consequences of assuming the death of the husband in the first case would be much more serious. The faraway husband, knowing that a writ of divorce sent by a messenger would have no validity, would refrain from sending one. As a result, his wife would become an *aguna*, neither married in fact nor able to remarry, since her husband might still be alive.

The "principle of the possible" is expressed in another, even more striking case, again concerning the levirate marriage and the *halitza* ceremony. According to biblical law, if the wife had given birth to a child before her husband died, the levirate marriage does not apply. This is true even if the child died immediately after birth. The rabbis, however, held that if the child was born prematurely, the birth is considered sufficient to disqualify the levirate marriage only if the newborn was fit for life. As to the question of what constitutes fitness for life, the Talmud offers two differing opinions. According to R. Shimon ben Gamliel, if the child lived for at least thirty days, we are certain that it was fully developed. But if it died within that period, there is a possibility that it was not quite fully developed. The rest of the rabbis, on the other hand, maintain that there is no need for a thirty-day period.

Assuming now that the widow remarried even though her child did not live thirty days, R. Shimon ben Gamliel would rule that because of the doubt regarding the child, she would still have to go through the *halitza* ceremony in order to be free of her ties to her former husband's brother. This may lead to unpleasant consequences, for there is a rule that a priest may not marry a woman "rejected" by means of *halitza*. Therefore it was decided that in case of a remarriage to an Israelite, we assume that the child was not viable, and therefore the woman must go through the ceremony. If she married a *kohen*, we assume that the child was completely developed; the mother is free to marry whomever she wants. In one instance we follow the opinion of R. Shimon ben Gamliel, in the other that of the other rabbis. How so? If she is married to an Israelite, the Talmud argues, "it is possible"; if she is married to a *kohen*, "it is not possible."

An Israelite may marry a woman who performed *halitza*; therefore, *halitza* is "possible." A priest is forbidden to marry such a woman; therefore, to require *halitza* is not "possible."[20]

In these examples the principle of the possible is explicitly used. In other cases it is not mentioned, but it is clearly the guiding consideration. On the Sabbath, for example, one is prohibited from leaving his city or community and walking in an undeveloped area beyond a distance of two thousand cubits. However, there are a number of exceptions to the rule. For instance, a midwife who is called to a delivery, a person needed to help fight a dangerous fire or to save people from a flood or from pirates, and so on—such are not only permitted but required to go wherever they are needed. However, a problem arises after they have completed the task to which they were called. According to the law, one who journeyed beyond the two-thousand-cubit limit must remain where he is until the end of the Sabbath. It is true that in our case the person was permitted to go beyond the Sabbath limit, but that was because of the emergency. Now that the emergency is over, is one tied down to the spot where he finds himself after the event? R. Gamliel the Elder, the head of the Sanhedrin, ruled that people who are allowed to travel for the sake of an emergency are to be considered as inhabitants of the city to which they have gone in order to help; like the latter, they too may move a distance of two thousand cubits in all directions. His reason was that if they were to be immobilized until the end of the Sabbath at the spot where they rendered help, they would not leave their homes to help in the first place. Thus, "the end was permitted on account of the beginning" is the talmudic formulation in this case.[21]

Similar considerations of the possible were obviously decisive in the formulation of two other principles. The halachic authorities have the power to restrict certain practices, out of a concern that they may lead to the violation of biblical commandments. However, no edicts of this kind may be issued if the majority of the people may not be able to obey them. Such edicts, if issued, lose their validity automatically.[22] Similarly, it was taught that if people engage in certain practices contrary to the obligations between man and God (the "ritual" commandments), and if there is reason to assume that reproving them will influence them to change their ways, one should do so. But if it cannot be assumed that they will change their ways if told that what they are doing is in violation of the law, then, says the Talmud, "Leave Israel alone; it is better that they should transgress out of ignorance than that they should do so intentionally." In one talmudic passage, it is said that this principle applies only to violations of rabbinic interdicts, but not in matters that the Bible itself forbids. A second passage, however, shows that it is valid even for biblical commandments.[23]

A careful examination of the examples discussed will show that in the application of the principle of the possible, the impossible is not the objectively impossible, but that which is not feasible. The category of the possible (*efshar*) represents that which, in view of human nature and with proper attention to human needs, is practically or morally feasible. Illustrations of pragmatic and moral feasibility are found in certain rules observed in the calculation of the annual calendar. Because of the difference between the solar and lunar years, it is necessary, at certain points within a multiyear cycle, to add an additional month, a second Adar, to the Jewish year. Apart from this, occasionally the second Adar was inserted for purely practical reasons that had nothing to do with the planetary order. And so it was taught:

> One introduces the additional month because of the roads, because of the bridges, because of the ovens for roasting the paschal lamb, and because of Jews who left their homes in exile [with the intention of going to Jerusalem to celebrate Passover there] but have not arrived yet.[24]

Because of the winter rains, the roads to Jerusalem were washed out, bridges were carried away by floods, ovens were damaged. It was, of course, a practical necessity to postpone the celebration of Passover by one month, so that the necessary repairs might be made. Most significant, however, is that it was postponed even in order not to disappoint travelers from Babylon who were on their way to celebrate the festival in Jerusalem but had been delayed, for whatever reason. The second Adar was added to the annual cycle of that year in order to enable them to arrive in time. The entire sequence of the year's holy days was thus moved by one month out of consideration for their feelings. To do anything else would have been "impossible," because it would not have been morally feasible.

The principle of moral feasibility is recognizable in other halachic decisions as well. Two examples are among the boldest. Guards of gardens and orchards are not obligated to fulfill the commandment of building a succah for the holiday of Succot. The discussion in the Talmud seems at first to assume that the reason for this is that since the orchards are usually outside the built-up areas, there are no festival booths available for the guards. Thus, the objection is raised: "Well, let them build their succah in the place where they keep watch." Upon which the answer is given: "The Bible says, 'you shall dwell in Succot': 'To dwell' means to live in them as one lives in one's home." But what does this mean? Explains Rashi: To dwell as one lives in one's home would require that the guards move into their festival booth in the orchard a great deal of their normal household—including beds, bedding, and other implements. It would put them to too much trouble. For this reason, they are freed from the obligation of dwelling in a succah.[25] The other ruling that attracts our attention deals with a specific aspect of the Yom Kippur observance. One of the five forms of abstinence that a Jew undergoes on the Day of Atonement pertains to washing. Apart from a minimum of cleaning the hands and eyes, among other pleasures one also forgoes on that day that of washing and bathing. According to some of the halachic authorities, this is a biblical command. However, one of the exceptions to the rule is a bride during the thirty days after her marriage. She may wash herself on Yom Kippur so that she should be beloved to her husband.[26] In both these cases, the morally feasible was the deciding factor.

Feasibility is clearly the main consideration in talmudic regulations in the economic field. A number of problems arose from the implementation of the biblical commandments regarding the sabbatical year. Every seventh year, no agricultural work was to be done in the fields and the gardens, and all debts were canceled. The cancellation of debts had serious economic consequences. As the seventh year approached, people would refuse to lend money to their fellows. Thus, the situation developed against which the Torah had warned:

> Beware that there be not a base thought in your heart, say-
> ing: "The seventh year, the year of release, is at hand"; and
> your eye be evil against your needy brother, and you give
> him nothing; and he cry unto the Eternal against you, and it
> be counted as a sin against you.[27]

Hillel saw that the entire purpose of the biblical injunction regarding the release of all debtors from their debts had
been foiled. He therefore introduced the regulation of *prozbul*,
according to which, as the seventh year approached, a creditor could hand over the promissory notes in his possession to a
rabbinical court, declaring that he himself would not demand
payment on them.[28] In this way, private debts in a sense became
public ones. Unlike the private creditor, the court did have the
right to demand payment, which it could then transfer to the
lender. As the Talmud explains, this regulation had a twofold
purpose, serving both the rich and the poor: The rich did not
lose their money; the poor, in need of a loan, were able to find
people who were willing to lend it to them.

The sabbatical year also caused other problems for the poor.
In other years, there was usually something for them from the
crops. They could go gleaning in the fields; any sheaf forgotten
was theirs by law. In addition, every farmer was obliged to leave
the corners of his field unharvested as the share of the poor. All
this was lost to them every seventh year. More serious was the
issue of unemployment. In a normal year they could hire themselves out for work with the farmers. In the sabbatical year, there
was no work for them in an agricultural society. This was a serious problem already at the time of the return of the Jews from
Babylon. As a solution, numerous areas that had previously been
Jewish land were excluded from the "sanctity" of the land of

Israel. Thus, in the sabbatical year, the poor would find work, as well as reaping the other benefits due them from the yield of the fields, in those districts.[29]

The problems caused by the sabbatical year pertained not only to the poor, but to society in general. Thus, the month that occasionally had to be added to the calendar was never introduced in a sabbatical year, but usually in the year immediately preceding it. On these occasions, astronomical calculations were disregarded. The reason was economic: Had the seventh year been thirteen months long, the period during which the land had to lie fallow would have been lengthened. This was to be avoided. But it was useful to lengthen the preceding year by one month, thereby allowing the farmers additional time to complete all their work in the fields.[30]

The Talmud relates that R. Yanai said to the people: "Go and sow in the seventh year because of the *arnona*," that is, the land tax that had to be paid to the non-Jewish authorities.[31] Had they not worked their land, they would not have been able to pay the tax. The commentaries endeavor to explain how R. Yanai could tell the people to violate a biblical commandment. Rashi maintains that R. Yanai must have believed that since the dispersion of the Jewish people, the sabbatical year had lost its status as a biblical commandment and was now only a rabbinical institution—a matter about which there is disagreement among the mishnaic teachers. Because of that, in times of need, it could be disregarded. The Tosafot, on the other hand, maintain that even if one is of the opinion that the sabbatical year still has biblical authority behind it, R. Yanai's message to the people may nevertheless be justified, for had they been unable to pay the required tax, they would have been imprisoned and might have been killed. It is, however, rather difficult to accept this explanation. The problem was not that of an individual but that of an entire community, and it is unlikely that they would all have been thrown into prison. More likely they would have been fined; perhaps part of their land would have been taken from them. All this might have created serious economic problems for the people. There is no proof at all of what R. Yanai's view was regarding the nature of the seventh-year observance. It need not surprise us that because of the grave economic consequences, he allowed the people to work their land in the sabbatical year, even if the commandment had retained its biblical authority over the course of time.

A number of other halachic arrangements were, in fact, amendments of biblical laws in response to economic needs. According to biblical law, the imposition of an oath on a litigant can only free him from payment. On the strength of an oath one can never gain payment for a claim. However, a modification of the rule was introduced in the case of a wage dispute. If a laborer claims that he did not receive his wages, and his claim is denied by the employer, in the absence of proof on either side, the laborer swears and receives his wages. The decision is based on two reasons. First, the wages are essential for the laborer's livelihood. Second, the laborer's claim is less likely to be mistaken than that of his employer. The laborer has only one employer, one wage to look forward to, whereas the employer often has many workers and is more occupied with his affairs than with each of his workers.[32]

Another modification of a rule concerning an oath is the following. If a person against whom a claim is made for payment of a loan admits to part of the claim, he has to take an oath that he does not owe the part that he denies, even when there is no evidence against him. But once again, an exception was allowed. What if someone finds a lost object and returns it to his owner, and the owner then claims that only a part of it was returned, and he demands full return? The finder need not take an oath to affirm his statement, even if he does admit to part of the claim against him. For if an oath were placed on the finder, people would not return lost objects.[33]

Let two more examples show how halachic innovations were introduced out of concern for the effective functioning of the "market." One example is actually called a "market regulation" (*takanat hashuk*).

> If one recognizes his implements or books in the possession of another, and it is known that they have been stolen from him, the one who bought the objects declares by oath how much he paid for them, and against payment the original owner receives his property back.[34]

It is, of course, assumed that the buyer was unaware that he had bought stolen goods. The goods were always the legal property of their original owner. Nevertheless, he has to buy them back. This was a regulation in order to protect the normal functioning of business transactions. As Rashi put it: "Since the buyer bought in the open market [without knowing that the goods were stolen], if the original owner would not return the price he paid, no one would dare buy anything for fear that it was stolen. Thus, all business would come to a standstill."[35]

A regulation regarding collateral was also formulated with a similar view to safeguarding the normal functioning of credit arrangements. It states that any loan issued on the basis of a promissory note automatically becomes a mortgage on the landed property of the borrower. In case of nonpayment, the creditor can collect the debt from the mortgaged property. This is true even if the property was sold to someone else in the interim; the buyer then has a claim against the original owner. However, if the loan was arranged orally, it does not become a mortgage on the borrower's property. In case of nonpayment, the creditor may not collect from any landed property that the borrower might have sold in the meantime.

This, however, is not the biblical law. There are two opinions recorded in the Talmud as to what the original biblical rule was in these matters. Ula is of the opinion that according to the Torah, all loans, whether in writing or by oral agreement, became mortgages on immobilia. Such a regulation, however, was commercially infeasible, for under the circumstances prevailing in talmudic times, only loans against an IOU, signed by two witnesses, became public knowledge. Therefore, anyone who bought any of the borrower's property would know of the existence of the loan and would be able to protect himself against the risk he was taking. But loans by oral agreement were completely private affairs, publicly unknown. However, since they, too, would mortgage property, a potential buyer would never know what chances he was taking. The result would destroy the realty market. For this reason, the halacha determined that only loans that became public knowledge, according to the circumstances of the times, became mortgages, but not the private ones granted by oral agreement only. Rabba, on the other hand, maintains that biblical law does not recognize that any kind of loan becomes a mortgage. But in that case, a creditor has no security for the money he lends. That would mean that people in need of credit would not be able to get it. This would greatly disorganize the economy. It was, therefore, decided that the creditor could receive a guarantee of repayment by insisting that he be given a duly executed promissory note, by which all landed property of the borrower became mortgaged to the creditor up to the amount of the loan.[36]

These halachic rulings to safeguard the efficient functioning of the economy correspond to a principle, derived from a biblical text, that "the Torah treats the money of Israel protectively." The talmudic rabbi Rava often made use of this principle in order to reach halachic decisions. In at least two cases he applied it as one of the arguments to rule in a question of food forbidden or permitted to be eaten.[37] In a similar discussion, R. Akiva called to his interlocutor: "How long will you waste the money of Israel?"[38] In a number of rulings, the course of leniency was chosen out of consideration of the financial damage that might accrue from an opposing view.[39]

All these rulings based on feasibility are not to be separated from moral considerations. The idea found its classical expression in a comment by R. Shimon concerning the festivals. As he explained it, the festivals of Passover and Succot last seven and eight days, respectively, but the festival of Shavuot lasts only one day. Why? In the spring, when Passover falls, as well as around Succot, after the harvest, there is little work in the fields; therefore, let them celebrate for eight days. But Shavuot falls in the busiest work season of the year. One day of festival will suffice. According to R. Shimon, in a spirit similar to that of the Torah's concern for the property of the people, this too teaches us that the Torah is protective toward Israel.[40] Concern about the material welfare of society is not materialism, but an expression of moral responsibility for the life of the people.

To illustrate the point further, it is worth concluding with an example from the Mishna. According to the Bible, a woman who gave birth brought a sacrifice to the Temple after the period of purification. If she could afford it, the sacrifice was a lamb "as a burnt offering" and a turtledove or pigeon "as a sin offering"; if she was poor, she brought another dove or pigeon in place of the lamb.[41] Now, if the woman failed to do this and went through a number of other births, she had to make offerings for each birth. For instance, after five births, she had to bring five such sacrifices. However, she did not have to bring them all at once. After the first sacrifice, she would be considered ritually pure again (meaning that she was permitted to partake of the meat of animals offered in the Temple). Now, apparently women often neglected to offer the prescribed sacrifice after every birth, so their sacrificial obligations accumulated. Women owed three, four, five, or more such sacrifices. In accordance with the law of supply and demand, the price of pigeons usually went up. As the Mishna tells it:

It happened once that the price for two such pigeons went up to a golden dinar. R. Shimon ben Gamliel, the head of the Sanhedrin, then took an oath and said: "I shall not go to bed tonight until the price goes down to a silver dinar." He went into the study house and taught: "A woman, even if she gives birth five times, brings only one sacrifice; the rest are no obligation upon her." Soon after, the price of the pigeons came down to half a silver dinar.[42]

Some of the commentaries are aghast. How could R. Shimon rule against the law? Rashi explains that even though R. Shimon was treating a biblical commandment lightly, it was an occasion "to act for the sake of God."[43] For if the prices did not go down, women would not bring even one sacrifice but would, nevertheless, eat of sacrificial meals in their ritual impurity. This was, indeed, one of these cases when one rules against the law for the sake of the law. But even Rashi, the great classical commentator on the plain meaning of all biblical and talmudic texts, was hesitant to accept the ruling of R. Shimon, as one may see from the fact that he had to give it a ritual justification—a reason for which there is not the slightest suggestion in the text. We are inclined to follow the view of Maimonides, who cites R. Shimon's declaration without any further comment.[44] In this case, we have before us a perfect combination of economic and moral feasibility. Preventing the exploitation of the poor was indeed acting for the sake of God.

THE PRIORITY OF THE ETHICAL

We have seen how interrelated pragmatic and moral considerations are in the halacha. In this section we will address the power of the ethical in the halacha. In his *Kuzari*, Judah Halevi writes: "God forbid that anything in the Torah should contradict reason." The rabbis in the Talmud were guided by the insight: God forbid that any application of the Torah to life should contradict the principles of ethics. What are those principles? They are Torah principles, such as: "And you shall do that which is right and good in the sight of the Eternal";[45] "Its ways are ways of pleasantness, and all its paths are peace" (according to talmudic teaching, this refers to the ways and the paths of the Torah);[46] or "That you may walk in the way of good people, and guard the paths of the righteous."[47]

In summation of such principles, the Talmud would say: "The Torah in its entirety exists for the sake of the ways of peace."[48] Quite clearly, these principles, and such an understanding of the meaning of the Torah, give priority to the ethical demand. In what follows I hope to show how this priority influences biblical interpretation, how it reaches out beyond strict legality, and how it even renders explicit biblical commandments inapplicable.

The festival of Succot is celebrated with the combination of the "Four Species." Two among them are the palm branch (*lulav*) and the myrtle boughs (*hadasim*). The Talmud, however, wishes to know why only the palm, and why only the myrtle? There are two other plants that would meet the exact meaning of the original Hebrew text of the Bible. In place of the palm, one could use the plant called *kufra*, and in place of the myrtle, another called *hirduf*. Answers Abaye: Neither of these plants could be meant, for it is written: "Its ways are ways of pleasantness." Explains Rashi: "*Kufra* is a thorny plant. Its many thorns would hurt the hands." The same applies to the *hirduf*. The ends of its leaves are sharp as needles; it would be difficult to handle it without being stuck by them. The Torah could not have meant those two plants, for it would not be in keeping with "ways of pleasantness." For the exclusion of the *hirduf*, Rava has another explanation: "The Bible could not have meant that plant, for it is written: 'You shall love truth and peace.'" Explains Rashi: "The *hirduf* is a plant from whose sap a lethal poison is distilled. The use to which this plant is put contradicts the idea of 'truth and peace.'"[49]

On the Sabbath one must not carry any kind of burden in a public domain. Thus the Mishna teaches: "A man should not walk out with a sword, bow and arrow, shield, spear, or lance." R. Eliezer disagreed. He was of the opinion that those weapons were an ornament for a man, and one may carry ornaments attached to the body on the Sabbath. The halacha was decided according to the other rabbis, who retorted to R. Eliezer: "Those weapons are nothing but a shame to man, for did not Isaiah prophesy that a time would come that 'the nations shall beat their swords into plowshares and their spears into pruning hooks; nation shall not lift up sword against nation, neither shall they learn war anymore'?"[50] If that is the ultimate ideal of universal history, the rabbis ask, how may weapons have any ornamental significance?

However, much more significant is the dominance of these principles in interpersonal relationships. Once again we refer to the laws governing the levirate marriage. It was the rule that a widow who had given birth to a child would marry outside the family of her former husband. If the child should die after her remarriage, even though there were no other offspring of her late husband, she need not go through the *halitza* ceremony in order to be released from her levirate bonds. From the point of view of talmudic reasoning, this was not at all obvious. A rule of talmudic deduction[51] is employed to argue that really the woman ought to perform *halitza*. But all logical reasoning is pushed aside by the statement that such could not be a law of the Torah, for it is said of the Torah: "Its ways are ways of pleasantness." In other words, it is inconceivable that the Torah would in this case require *halitza*. The woman is already married. To subject her to such a ceremony would be humiliating for her vis-à-vis her present husband.[52]

The reference to the overruling ethical principle is not always explicit in halachic decisions. It is, however, obvious that it plays a decisive role in the final conclusion. People ignorant of Judaism quote "an eye for an eye, a tooth for a tooth" as a principle of Judaic justice. Apart from the fact that the translation itself is questionable, the halachic interpretation as early as the mishnaic period (ending around 200 C.E.) concluded that the Bible was referring to monetary compensation. The effort made to justify this interpretation is most impressive. Almost all the arguments are of an ethical nature. For instance, if you take "an eye for an eye" literally, then the law itself becomes inapplicable: Surely, "an eye for an eye," but not an eye for an eye and a life. But occasionally, by taking a man's eye one may be taking much more than that, depending on the success of the operation or on the state of health of the person involved; it may even cost him his life. Therefore, the Bible can mean only monetary compensation for an eye or a tooth. Whatever the logical validity of the arguments, the halachic decision was not literally an eye for an eye, but payment of damages for the eye lost.[53]

A similar reinterpretation of the plain, literal meaning of the biblical text is given in another connection. The Bible says that if an ox was "wont to gore in the past, and warning has been given to its owner, and he has not kept it in, but it has killed a man or a woman; the ox shall be stoned and its owner also shall be put to death."[54] Once again the halachic teachers, with the help of other relevant biblical passages, ruled that monetary damages to be paid to the family were meant, for "one puts a person to death if he himself kills, but not if his ox kills."[55] It is quite obvious that independently of all adduced "corroborative" biblical material, the halachic conscience could not accept the idea that a man, though not guiltless (he had after all been warned about the wildness of his animal), should be put to death for the goring of his ox.

The halachic humanization of the textual regulations governing the punishment of flogging, prescribed for certain transgressions, is illuminating. First of all, it was decided that flogging was to be carried out with a strap made from the skin of a calf, which is much softer than one made from the skin of a full-grown animal. Second, it was shown that the forty stripes that the Bible prescribes were really only thirty-nine. This is important, because it was further shown that the flogging was not to be administered to one part of the body, but had to be divided into three parts: one part to the front of the body, and two parts to be divided between each of the shoulders.

The consequences of this tripartite division could be rather significant. Prior to punishment, the condemned person would be examined in order to decide how many lashes his body could endure without harming his health. If the experts determined that he could endure no more than twenty, he would be given only eighteen (because twenty is not divisible into three parts), to be distributed equally among three sections of the body. The officers who administered the punishment had to be physically weak but of keen intelligence. They needed to be able to discern, as they proceeded, whether the ordered number of lashes was too much for the health of the transgressor.

Finally, there was also a law that if the original judgment was for thirty-nine stripes, but in the course of flogging it was noticed that the person could not tolerate more than twenty, the flogging had to stop. On the other hand, if he was condemned to twenty lashes, and as the punishment was given it became evident that he could very well endure the full measure of thirty-nine, the punishment had to stop nonetheless in accordance with the original estimate. Rashi explains: "Once a person has received a flogging, even if not the prescribed number of lashes, he has been humiliated for his transgression. That is enough." The idea has its basis in a strange biblical formulation that states, at the end of the description of the punishment, "and your brother shall be dishonored before your eyes."[56] The word "dishonored" in Hebrew (*nikleh*) strongly suggests another word that has the same letters and with a slight change in the order of the letters means "be beaten" (*nilkeh*). The rabbis took the hint and interpreted: "Once he has been humiliated [for his transgression], he again becomes your brother."[57]

All the above rulings are somehow based on textual interpretation. But quite clearly, it is the halachic conscience that creates the interpretation.

The halacha was not very comfortable with the idea of corporal punishment. There was an element of insult in it to the dignity of man. And the concern for respect for the individual (*kevod habriot*) is an authentic halachic principle. Its corrective implication in matters of biblical law is derived from the Bible itself. The Torah orders that if an animal, even one belonging to one's enemy, collapses under the weight of its burden, one is obligated to help the owner lift the goods from its back. By the midrashic method of interpretation, it is concluded that an old man or a scholar for whom it is not befitting to engage in such menial efforts is exempted from this obligation. The exemption is then formulated as a halachic principle: "Great is the importance of a person's honor, for it overrides a biblical commandment."[58]

The same principle is applied in an entirely different case. According to biblical law, a member of the priestly caste, for reasons of ritual purity, must not have any contact with a dead body (except that of a close relative). However, when a corpse is found and there is no one to attend to its burial other than a priest, he is obligated to bury the dead. The reason is the same: "Great is the importance of a person's honor, for it overrides a biblical commandment." Only this time, the honor is the respect due to the dead. Nonetheless, the dignity of man is being protected. In the Babylonian Talmud, the general validity of the overriding power of this principle is limited to monetary regulations. (The case of the *met mitzva*, the person who dies and has no one to take care of his burial, is considered an exception.) In all other matters, only rabbinical laws may be superseded by consideration for respect for the individual. The Jerusalem Talmud makes much greater use of this principle. Occasionally, it overrides there even biblical commandments in non-monetary matters.[59]

In cases where there was no question that the written word might impinge on the human dignity of a person, the halacha was mindful not to allow practices that would shame the ignorant and, especially, the poor. The Bible prescribes the reading of an appropriate text at the annual offering of the first fruits at the Temple in Jerusalem. Originally, those who could read would read the verses themselves. Someone else would read on behalf of those who could not. However, this practice shamed the illiterate, and they refused to come. Thus, a new regulation was introduced: An official of the Temple had to read the prescribed text on behalf of everyone without distinction.[60]

A more significant example: During the Temple period, a great many laws of ritual purity were in effect. At the same time, it was known that an *am ha'aretz*, a Jew ignorant of the Torah (a rather incomplete description of the type, but sufficient for our purpose), was not too careful in observing the laws of purity. Therefore, a scholarly observant Jew would not eat food or drink wine touched by an *am ha'aretz*. However, an exception was made during the three annual pilgrimage festivals. During the festival period, all Jews were treated as if they were scholars. This meant that the foods and wines in the stores, which were, of course, handled by the many pilgrims, including numerous ignorant ones, were all deemed "pure," permissible to be used by a scholar. Were the reasons for the exemption economic? Rashi explains that discrimination against the ignorant on those occasions would have been a public insult to them—meaning that one would have had to declare publicly to beware of all food touched by an *am ha'aretz*, or, perhaps, special stores for them would have had to be established.[61]

A number of regulations regarding customs of mourning and burial were guided by considerations of respect for the feelings of the poor. The rabbis taught:

Originally, the food [traditionally brought to the house of the mourner after the funeral] was brought to the rich in silver and gold baskets, and to the poor in baskets made of stripped willow twigs. The poor were ashamed. Because of the honor of the poor, it was ordered that one would have to come to all homes with twig baskets. Originally, in the houses of the rich the drinks would be offered to the mourners in costly white glass; for the poor, they would use cheap, colored glass. The poor were ashamed. Because of the honor of the poor, it was ordered that in all homes only colored glass was to be used.

Originally, the faces of the dead of the rich would be uncovered [for the funeral]. The faces of the poor would be covered, however, because they often showed the signs of starvation. The poor were ashamed. Because of the honor of the poor, it was ordered that at all funerals the face of the dead was to be covered. Originally, the dead of the rich would be carried to their burial on couches; but of the poor in cheap, wooden boxes. The poor were ashamed. Because of the honor of the poor, it was ordered that all dead were to be carried in boxes.

Originally, the apparel in which the dead were clothed for the funeral was so expensive that the poor could not afford it, so that [it was said] it was harder for them to raise the money than even to bear their sorrow for the dead. They would leave the body and run away. Until R. Gamliel, the head of the Sanhedrin, ordered "irreverent" treatment of himself, that he be carried out in a cheap, cotton shroud. After that, the people followed his example, and they too used cheap shrouds made from cotton.[62]

On happy occasions, too, social behavior was guided by sensitivity toward the poor. It is told that there were no holidays in Israel like the fifteenth of Av and Yom Kippur. It seems that on those two days, a popular festival took place that enabled the daughters of Israel to go out and look for suitable husbands in all modesty. The happy mood of the festival was due to the fact that girls did not go out in fashionable clothes according to the financial status of the family. They all had to dress in borrowed, white garments, including the daughters of the king. Everyone had to borrow from someone lower on the social and financial scale than oneself. This was the rule, in order "not to embarrass those who did not have any" nice clothing.[63]

Often, in the area of interpersonal relationships, corrective innovation had to be employed with respect to the law. This correction was necessary because the law is always general. Its very generality, however, is at times unable to do justice to the particular or specific. For example, certain laws determine the formal requirements for the legal transfer of property. One form of acquisition is by way of one's yard: Any object placed in a yard with the intention of transferring it into the possession of the yard's owner is legally acquired. This form of acquisition was extended to include the case of any ownerless object or valuable that lies in (certain) areas within a radius of four cubits from where one is standing. The regulation was introduced that whatever is found within that space becomes the property of the person standing there. This was done in order to eliminate quarrels between people. If a more technical form of taking possession were required in such cases, it would very often lead to quarrels, for instance. If one person was bending down to take hold of an object lying in front of him, and someone else anticipated him by a quick movement. In order to reduce such cases to a minimum, the rabbinical regulation (*takana*) was introduced.[64]

Other innovations were instituted in order to prevent hatred
between people. We shall cite only one example among many.
According to R. Yehuda Hanasi, the editor of the authoritative
version of the Mishna, a person could legally betroth a married woman on the condition that she become his wife after the
death of her husband. Similarly, since according to biblical law
(even in times of polygamy) one was not permitted to marry
his wife's sister, he could conclude a marriage contract with a
woman on the condition that she become his wife after the death
of her sister, the present wife. In general, such agreements had,
according to R. Yehuda Hanasi, full legal force. According to
the law, therefore, in case of the death of the sister, the marriage
thus concluded would take effect automatically. Yet the rabbis
ruled that in these cases the general law did not apply. Marriage
arrangements of this nature would lead to enmity between husband and wife, between sister and sister, between one man and
another. This consideration invalidated a marriage contract that
was legally binding according to biblical law.[65]

A great many regulations were introduced because of the
"ways of peace." Some of them deal with relationships to non-
Jews. "The rabbis taught: Because of the ways of peace, one is
obligated to support the Gentile poor together with the Jewish
poor; to visit the Gentile sick as one visits the Jewish sick; to
bury the non-Jewish dead as one buries the dead among Jews."
In another passage it was added that one should comfort Gentile
mourners, as demanded by the "ways of peace."

Another group of regulations instituted because of the "ways
of peace" are actual deviations from the generality of the law.
Animals, birds, and fish that are caught in traps and nets do not
become legally acquired property as long as they remain in the

traps or nets. One can acquire property by placing it in any container, but neither a trap nor a net is considered a receptacle that holds objects as a container. Nevertheless, it was ruled that for a stranger to remove the catch from them would be equal to robbery. A similar case: Children and the mentally ill are not legally authorized to acquire property. If they found a lost object, it would not pass into their possession, and anyone could come and take it away from them. However, it was ruled that to do so would be robbery. In these examples, the rabbis went against the law or beyond it because of the importance of the "ways of peace." In fact, it was in the context of all such regulations that the statement was made that the entire Torah is "for the sake of the ways of peace."[66]

In cases that are not directly related to social peace, the halacha urges the Jew to forgo certain advantages that he might gain from a strict adherence to the law. In interpersonal relationships, this is known as "the deed that they should do." Leniency and generosity toward fellow human beings are urged upon the Jew by the rabbinical interpretation of certain passages in the Torah.

Earlier in this chapter, we saw that out of respect for their honored status, old men and scholars are not obligated to help raise an animal that has collapsed under its burden. Yet at the same time, these respected people are urged not to make use of the exception and to act in accordance with the law that is generally binding for all, but to remain "within the line of the law" (*lifnim mishurat hadin*), even though legally they could go further. This regulation applies to all situations in which, because of special circumstances, one is freed from obligations toward another person that normally would be binding. Thus, the same

Torah that grants the exemption also urges the Jew not to take advantage of it.[67]

In other cases, the halacha not only urges a person not to insist on rights which are his by law, but obligates him to forgo them. According to the law, a person may sell his property to whomever he wishes, and so anyone has the right to buy any property that is for sale. Yet this right was limited by the "law of bordering property" (*dina devar metzra*). When someone wishes to sell a tract of land, the owner of the property bordering on that land has the prerogative of buying it. If it was not offered to him first but was sold to someone else, the buyer has to return the land to the neighbor, who reimburses the buyer according to the price he paid for it. The reason given is that the Torah says: "And you shall do that which is right and good in the sight of the Eternal."[68] To appreciate the significance of what we have called creative interpretation, it is worth recalling the context in which these words occur:

> You shall diligently keep the commandments of the Eternal your God, and the testimonies and statutes which he has commanded you. And you shall do that which is right and good in the sight of the Eternal...[69]

The teachers of the halacha did not read these verses as having only one meaning: Do the right and the good by keeping my commandments. The words "you shall do that which is right and good" were understood as an additional commandment. In addition to observing the laws of the Torah, also do that which is right and good. This could mean that it is sometimes necessary to go beyond the law, which in itself is right and good, in order to do what is right and good.

A case that caused some confusion among the talmudic commentators in these matters is the following. Some workers hired by Rabba bar Bar Hana dropped a barrel of wine and caused him considerable damage. According to the laws of damages, the workers were responsible and obligated to pay. Rabba bar Bar Hana took away some of their clothing, either to ensure payment or in lieu of it. They turned to Rav for help. He ordered that their clothes be returned to them. Rabba bar Bar Hana asked: "Is this the law?" Rav answered: "Yes, for it is written: 'That you may walk in the way of good people.'" He returned their clothes but did not pay their wages. Once again they turned to Rav, saying: "We are poor people. We have toiled all day. We are hungry and have nothing"—upon which Rav ordered Rabba bar Bar Hana to pay their wages. Once again he asked: "Is this the law?" and was answered: "Yes, for it is written [in the second part of the same verse]: 'And guard the paths of the righteous.'"[70]

The commentators struggle with the question of whether this was indeed the law or only a form of moral admonishment addressed by Rav to Rabba bar Bar Hana. Rashi and others accept the latter opinion; but there are also halachic authorities who maintain that Rav gave a legally enforceable ruling. A comparison with a similar story in the Jerusalem Talmud may help us to appreciate better the significance of the story as told in the Babylonian one. There we read that R. Nehemia the potter handed some of his pots to a worker, who then broke them; R. Nehemia took the man's clothing as a deposit against payment. The man took the case to R. Yose bar Hanina. He advised him to go back to R. Nehemia and tell him: "That you may walk in the way of good people." When R. Nehemia heard this, he gave back the clothes. But he did not pay the man's wages. So R. Yose told him: "Go back and quote him the second half of the verse: 'And guard the paths of the righteous.'" When R. Nehemia heard this, he paid the man his wages.[71]

This is clearly not the same case history told differently in the Babylonian Talmud. Such occurrences obviously happened quite often. The differences in style between the two narratives are considerable. R. Yose does not give instruction directly to R. Nehemia but advises the laborer how to appeal to him. R. Nehemia could have refused to be moved by the plea. Not so in the story in the Babylonian Talmud. There, Rav does not give advice; he pronounces law. There is a direct encounter between himself and the employer, upon whose challenge Rav insists: Yes, this is the law. Quite clearly, there is a difference here between the Jerusalem view and the Babylonian view. According to the former, to "walk in the way of good people and guard the paths of the righteous" is a moral injunction that contradicts the law of damages and is not enforceable. The Babylonian view, however, is that with all due respect to the law of damages, there are cases when it is overruled by a superior ethical principle that, in those cases, becomes itself the overriding law.

In the foregoing example, the law in its generality was sustained, and only its application in exceptional cases was limited. Occasionally, however, the ethical conscience of halacha weakened the very purpose of the law and even declared it to be inoperative. One of these laws concerns the status of the "bastard" (*mamzer*). According to the Bible, "A bastard shall not enter into the congregation of the Eternal."[72] This means that a bastard can marry only another bastard. He is not permitted into the family community of the Jewish people. It is important to understand that the bastard referred to in the Bible is not the illegitimate child of Western civilization. A child born to an unmarried woman is, according to the halacha, fully legitimate. Rather, a bastard (*mamzer*) is the offspring of a biblically forbidden union, such as adultery or incest.

The law intended to discourage such unions, to cause the parties to think of the very severe consequences for the child born of them. But those very consequences for the innocent child caused the rabbis a great deal of ethical discomfort. They expressed their moral reservations in the form of a midrashic interpretation of a verse in Ecclesiastes. This is the biblical text:

> So I returned and considered all the oppressions that are done under the sun. And behold the tears of the oppressed, and they had no comforter. And on the side of their oppressors there was power, but they had no comforter.[73]

The midrash asks who is meant by "the oppressed." All kinds of answers are given. In the end we hear the interpretation of Daniel the tailor. He maintains that the author has the bastards in mind.

> "Behold the tears of the oppressed." Their fathers sinned, but what has it to do with these insulted ones? The father of this one went to a woman forbidden to him, but how did the child sin, and how does it concern him? They "had no comforter," but "on the side of their oppressors there was power." Those are the hands of the Great Sanhedrin, which move against them with the authority of the Torah

and remove them from the community, because it is written: "A bastard shall not enter into the congregation of the Eternal." "And they had no comforter." Therefore, says the Holy One: "It is upon me to comfort them." In this world there are those among them who are unworthy; but regarding the messianic era, Zechariah prophesied: "Behold I see them all like pure gold"; for this is symbolized by his vision: "I saw, and behold, it was an oil lamp of pure gold."[74]

With greater simplicity, it is said in the Talmud in the name of R. Yose, whose opinion is accepted, that "in the days of the Messiah, bastards... will be pure."[75]

One follows with astonishment the boldness of these rabbis, who certainly believed that the law of the Torah was divine and yet criticized it in the name of God, as it were. In their words, God himself realizes that this law has to be changed. The "bastards" too will be declared pure. God himself will comfort them. We ought to see, however, that the criticism is also based on the Bible, for the Bible deplores the injustice done to the oppressed, whose tears are disregarded, and who are surrendered into the hands of the established authorities. On the other hand, what is the Great Sanhedrin to do? They function by the power entrusted to them by the Torah.

This is one of those situations in which the halacha is called in to function. There is a law whose purpose is a positive one; namely, to protect the moral health of the family. But there is also a biblical view of the seriousness of the injustice done to innocent people in general. And in this specific case innocent people suffer because of the valid concern and care for the ethical foundations of the community. It is as if the happiness of the bastard were sacrificed to a greater good. It was unquestionably an injustice done to an innocent human being.

The halachic way out of the dilemma was a very circumspect application of the law of the illegitimate child. First, there is the ruling of R. Yitzhak that in the case of a family in which a bastard has "submerged" (that is, his status as such is not publicly known), we let him be submerged—one does not make investigations to discover who is a bastard and who is not (as Rashi mentions, in any case in the end all families will be declared pure). On the basis of this ruling, R. Yohanan, one of the leading sages of the Jerusalem Talmud (often quoted also in the Babylonian one), took an oath that he could easily prove the presence of bastards in some families in the land of Israel. "But," said he, "what can I do? Some of the great men of this generation are among them." Again, the same situation emerges: The application of the law concerning bastards could not be the only consideration. The law was not applied because of weightier considerations. Finally, while the law giving expression to an idea that was in itself meaningful was acknowledged, it was also decided that it was forbidden for anyone to reveal that someone is an illegitimate child.[76]

Much more far-reaching were the results of the halachic conscience in some other conflicts with the written law. One example was the case of the "stubborn and rebellious son" who was "a glutton and a drunkard" and did not listen to the voice of his parents. If his father and mother together agreed that there was no other recourse for them but to hand him over to the "elders of the city," then, says the Bible, he should be put to death. "So shall you put away the evil from your midst; and all Israel shall hear and fear."[77]

One may judge such a law rather cruel. From the beginning it required justification. It was said that the "stubborn and rebellious son" was put to death because of his threatening end. The Torah understood where his ways were leading him. He would consume the property of his father. Finally, not finding the means to satisfy his addictions, he would become a highway robber. Said the Torah: Let him die while he is still innocent, rather than later, when he is guilty.

The regulations attached to the law by the teachers of the halacha were so numerous and so meticulous that even if one had followed the biblical injunction, in practice the law would have been implemented only very seldom. In fact, R. Shimon, one of the halachic authorities of the mishnaic period, declared that a case of the "stubborn and rebellious son" never happened and would never happen. The reason he gave had nothing to do with halacha. For "because this son ate meat equal to the value of a *tartemor* [an ancient Greek coin] and drank half a *log* [a large liquid measure] of fine Italian wine, his parents would hand him over to be stoned to death?" Such things do not happen. The law may say what it pleases; it has no application in human experience.

Another mishnaic teacher, R. Yehuda, went even further. He "interpreted" the biblical text in such a manner as to show that if you followed its literal meaning, it would hardly be possible to make any use of this law. According to the text, the parents have to appear before the elders and declare: "This our son is stubborn and rebellious; he does not hearken to our voice; he is a glutton and a drunkard." Commented R. Yehuda:

"Does not hearken to our voice," says the Bible. "Voice" is in the singular. Now, a father and mother may agree on this matter and speak as if with one voice, but in actual fact they each have a voice of their own. But the Bible says, "our voice"; it can mean only that their voices are alike also in the physical sense. But if their voices must be indistinguishable, then it means that the parents also have to be alike physically in appearance and height. All these conditions, of course, can never be met. Therefore, it never happened, nor will it ever happen.

And now follows the most surprising conclusion of this entire discussion. "If so," R. Yehuda asks, "why was it written?" The answer is: "To interpret it [showing that it was not meant to be implemented] and to receive divine reward for its study."[78] It is as if it were a test of the intelligence and the conscience of the student and the teacher.

A similar "interpretation" was given to another law of the Torah. The Bible decreed that if an entire city was led astray to idol worship by some of its inhabitants, it was to be destroyed, including its inhabitants and all their property. The law expressed Judaism's desperate struggle against polytheism. Faith in the one God was the *raison d'être* of Jewish existence. Without monotheism there could be no Jewish people. Yet to destroy an entire city was not an easy matter. Thus we hear that this law was never enacted. "The case of the 'city led astray'—it never was, nor will it ever be." How so? The answer given is that the Bible commands: "And you shall gather all its spoil into its broad place, and shall burn the city with fire…."[79] Now it is impossible that at least one of the doorposts in the condemned city should not have a *mezuza* (a parchment scroll containing verses of the Bible) attached to it. But since it contains the name of God, a *mezuza* must not be burned. The commandment says: "And you shall gather *all* its spoil" and burn it. This law cannot be fulfilled. Part of the "spoil" would be *mezuzot*, and they cannot be burned. Therefore, this commandment was given "in order to be 'interpreted' and to be rewarded" for an interpretation that shows that the law was never meant to be applied.[80]

One might say that in all these cases—the "bastard," the "stubborn and rebellious son," and the "city led astray"—the law intends mainly to impress the importance of an idea upon the consciousness of the Jewish people. There are, however, many other examples of rulings that are meant either to limit or even to frustrate completely the implementation of the law in actual life situations.

The halachic authorities were extremely hesitant about imposing the death penalty, even though it is provided for in biblical law. Thus, the Mishna rules: "A Sanhedrin that condemned even just one person to death in seven years was called a killer court." This tradition was corrected by a mishnaic teacher to read, "once in seventy years." Finally we hear the words of R. Yishmael and R. Akiva, who said: "Had we been there [i.e., had we been members of the Sanhedrin], no one would ever have been put to death."[81] (They lived after the legislative authority of the Sanhedrin had already lapsed.) The Talmud explains that they would have found reasons to show why the death penalty could not be imposed. Once again we find a tension between the written law and the living conscience. The law is not to be abolished. It is the law of the Torah. And, indeed, there are crimes and sins for which one may well deserve the death penalty. But whether to put a human being to death by human hands is another matter. When R. Yishmael and R. Akiva declared that they would not have done it, their decision was also based on the teachings of the Torah. For halachic reasons, based on the Torah, this biblical law, valid in itself, would not be put into practice.

THE EXAMPLE OF MARRIAGE AND DIVORCE LAW

It is doubtful whether the halachic conscience is anywhere more strongly in evidence than in the area of the marriage and divorce laws. In these matters we find a full understanding of the legal weakness of the status of the woman. As is the way of the halacha, great efforts are made to retain the meaning of the legal principle and yet to find solutions to the daily problems arising from the confrontation between the written word and the moral demands of the concrete situation.

Some of the halachic rulings deal with the laws of marriage (*kidushin*); most of them deal with those of divorce (*gitin*). According to the law, a man may enter into marriage by authorizing another person to betroth a woman on his behalf by the prescribed ceremony. But Rav, the most respected halachic authority in Babylon, forbade marrying a woman by proxy. His reason was that when the man meets his wife, he might find her disagreeable. But the Torah commanded: "You shall love your neighbor as yourself."[82] One who marries by proxy exposes himself to a situation in which he will not be able to fulfill the commandment of loving his wife as himself.[83] A similar ruling of Rav (or, according to another opinion, of R. Elazar) concerned the marriage of minors. For social reasons, in conditions that no longer prevail, the Bible authorized a father to marry off a daughter who is a minor to whomever he pleased. According to the later ruling, the practice of this law was forbidden. The halachic authorities ruled that a father may marry off a minor only if she explicitly declares that she is willing to marry the person her father chooses for her.[84]

Neither were the rabbis satisfied with the legal situation of the married woman. Biblical law mentions a threefold obligation of the husband toward his wife. He must provide her with food and clothing and must respect her conjugal rights. In the rabbis' view, this was inadequate. Thus, they introduced the formal marriage contract, or *ketuba*, in which the mutual obligations of the marriage partners are set out, among them a sum of money that the husband has to pay his wife should he divorce her. With the introduction of the marriage contract, all kinds of conditions were routinely included in writing: For instance, the husband's obligation to pay for medical treatment in case of the wife's illness, to pay ransom should she be kidnapped, to pay for all burial expenses, and to arrange for her to be maintained by his estate as long as she remained a widow.[85] All these were revolutionary innovations introduced no later than the mishnaic period.

The most significant aspect of the introduction of the marriage contract was that it established the halachic possibility of including all kinds of other conditions in the marriage agreed upon by the parties. The payment to the wife in case of divorce, provided for in the set formula of the contract, could be increased as a condition of the marriage. In times and places of polygamous practices, the bride could demand that the contract contain the condition that the groom obligate himself not to take another wife. It could also be clearly stated what the consequences would be if the husband broke the agreement. The marriage contract was meant to strengthen the status of the woman and to see to it that it should not be easy for the husband to divorce her. R. Meir declared that it was forbidden to marry without a contract. The conditions introduced by the halachic authorities as the minimal norm for every marriage were assumed to be automatically implied in every marriage contract and were binding upon both partners even if they were not explicitly set out in the *ketuba*.[86]

There is at least one case in which the halacha denies a husband his right to divorce his wife: When the woman is insane. This was a complete departure from biblical law. Legally a husband may divorce his insane wife as long as she understands the meaning of the divorce. This was interpreted to mean that after she is handed the writ of divorce, she does not return to the house of her husband. Now, it may occur that such a woman is capable of understanding what a divorce is but is completely incompetent to look after herself. In talmudic language, she can keep her writ but cannot keep herself. The rabbis ruled that such a woman must not be divorced, that she may not become treated as one abandoned. She remains a married woman, and her husband must take care of her.[87]

One area in which the woman was most severely disabled was that of divorce. There she was completely in the power of her husband. Whereas the husband could divorce his wife at any time at will, she could not divorce him. The matter was further complicated by the fact that a writ of divorce, or *get*, given by the husband under duress was invalid. Often this law is morally

intolerable. The Mishna suggests a way out: "These are the husbands whom we compel to divorce their wives: A person with
severe boils, one suffering from a bad odor from the nose, the
worker whose task it is to collect the excrement of dogs, a cop-
per miner, and a tanner."

Apart from the first, in all these cases the reason is that a
bad odor is attached to the people who suffer from those ill-
nesses or earn their livelihood in such a manner. It was assumed
that one may not compel the wife to stay with her husband in
those circumstances. R. Meir is of the opinion that the wife may
insist upon a divorce even if she knew prior to the marriage of
the condition of her husband or his work and agreed explicitly to enter into the marriage with him in spite of it. She may
plead: "I thought I could endure it; now I see that I cannot."
While the majority opinion did not take R. Meir's view, there is
general agreement among the talmudic teachers that one compels the husband to divorce his wife if the circumstances of his
bodily state were not known to her prior to the marriage. The
commentators understood that "to compel" here means even
by physical punishment.[88] (In our day it would probably mean
imprisonment.)

But does not biblical law state that the *get* has to be handed
to the wife of the husband's free will? A way out of this dilemma
was found by the surprisingly original idea that since it is right
and proper that a husband divorce his wife in such a case, if he
refuses to do so, "we compel him until he declares: Yes, I do
wish to divorce her." This, of course, requires explanation. In his
code, Maimonides cites the ruling as follows:

> Whenever the law requires that a husband be ordered to
> divorce his wife, and he refuses to do so, the Jewish court in

any place and at all times imposes corporal punishment on him until he says, "I am willing"; he writes the *get*, and it is valid. Similarly, if he is thus compelled by a non-Jewish court that orders him to act as demanded by the rabbinical court, and the Jews are pressuring him through Gentile hands until he divorces his wife, the divorce is valid. And why does such a divorce not become invalid? After all, he is forced to act against his will, regardless of whether it is by the rabbinical or the non-Jewish court. [The answer is] that we consider compulsion only if one is forced to do something that the Torah does not obligate him to do.... But one who is driven by his evil inclination to nullify a positive commandment or to commit a sin and is then compelled until he agrees to do what he is obligated to do... is not considered to have been forced. It is he who forced himself by his evil intent.[89]

The first impression one may gain from this "explanation" is that Maimonides is of the opinion that the punishment frees the husband from the clutches of his evil inclination, so that he may be free to act as he really wants. The idea becomes somewhat more sympathetic in its concluding elaboration. This is how Maimonides sums it up:

Therefore this man who does want to divorce his wife, since he does want to be a Jew and does want to fulfill all the commandments and avoid all sins, and since it is his evil urge that overwhelmed him at the moment, if as the result of his punishment his urge has been weakened, and he is therefore able to say, "I am willing," he then divorces his wife out of his own will.[90]

Assuming that we are dealing with a person who lives according to Torah law, and therefore approves in principle of the halacha that orders husbands to divorce their wives in certain situations, it does make sense to say that this husband who refuses to obey the rules of the Torah because it affects him personally is indeed his own prisoner.

In somewhat more general terms, one might say that as long as a person is a member of a society and does not leave it, *eo ipso* he obligates himself to adhere to its laws. He freely surrenders his freedom in all matters in which the law imposes its discipline. Occasionally, coercion is needed to remind him of the terms of his membership. In less legalistic language and closer to contemporary ideas about the truth that "man is to freedom condemned," one might also say that a human being is always confronted with choices. He may rebel against the laws of his society, in which case he chooses to face the consequences of his rebellion. If the society then punishes him as the law provides, that was his choice. If, on the other hand, he decides to give up his rebellion and because of the pressure of the punishment obeys the law, that too was his choice. He acts as he does now because he has chosen obedience over rebellion. Be that as it may, the important thing here is that there were situations in which one could not expect a woman to continue in marriage. A way was found to dissolve that marriage, a way not originally provided for in the law.

There are a number of other cases in which the husband is to be urged, or even compelled, to divorce his wife freely. We shall discuss only two more examples here, that of the "rebellious husband" and that of the "rebellious wife." On the basis of the corresponding talmudic sources, the *Shulhan Aruch* rules as follows:

If a husband rebels against his wife and says, "I will provide for her sustenance, but I refuse conjugal relationship with her because I hate her," then [at first] one adds weekly... to her *ketuba* [i.e., to the sum the husband has to pay her in case of divorce], and she may continue living with him so long as she desires. But although the value of her *ketuba* increases continually, the husband is still violating a biblical commandment [by denying her conjugal rights].... Thus, if she wishes, one compels him immediately to divorce her and pay her *ketuba*.[91]

Even more significant is the halachic ruling in the case of the "rebellious wife." Here it is the woman who refuses to have conjugal relations with her husband. The talmudic statement on the subject is ambiguous; it allows two interpretations. Among the classical commentators, some are of the opinion that in such a case one compels the husband to grant his wife a divorce. The most sympathetic view in this matter seems to be that of Maimonides. He cites the law as he understands the relevant statement in the Talmud and adds to it his own personal reason for the law, one not mentioned explicitly in the talmudic sources:

A woman who refuses conjugal contact with her husband is called "rebellious." One has to ask her why she rebels. If she says: "I dislike him and cannot have intercourse with him," one compels her husband to divorce her. She is not like a captive woman [the reference is to the law regarding the enemy woman captured in a war, discussed earlier], that she should submit to one she dislikes.[92]

Some of the leading halachic authorities agree with the decision of Maimonides. Others who interpret the relevant talmudic text differently disagree with him. The discussion shows that the vehement disagreement with Maimonides is based not so much on the talmudic source material as on personal apprehension of the conditions to which the view of Maimonides may lead. If a husband can be coerced to divorce a "rebellious wife," then any woman who "set her eyes on another man" could claim that she could not endure her husband and would thus get a divorce.[93] Obviously this is no solution to the problem. The argument against Maimonides perceives an easy way out for the *prutza*, the dissolute woman, if his opinion were adopted. Of course, the real problem exists not for the *prutza* but, on the contrary, for the honest woman. The more honest she is, the less is she able to continue living with a husband with whom she is incompatible.

Much greater understanding for the plight of the "rebellious wife" is shown by a halachic authority whom one of the medieval commentators calls "the rabbi," without mentioning his name. The rabbi does not fully share the view of Maimonides, but neither does he accept the opinion of his opponents. Whereas it is generally assumed that the rebellious wife, if she is divorced, loses the monetary compensation set out in the marriage contract, the rabbi writes as follows:

If she says she dislikes him, one does not compel her to stay with him by warning her about the loss of the value of her *ketuba*. One leaves her to her attitude [toward her husband]. Since her husband is displeasing to her, she is like one coerced in the matter. She cannot help herself. Even a good and pious woman cannot submit to a husband whom she rejects... even if no faults are visible in him. Such things happen quite often. This is not unlike the case of a person who is unable to eat a certain kind of food that is detestable to him. There is no way here to coerce her. One should rather intercede with her, to influence her to accept him. Furthermore, if we were sure that what she says was true, that he is indeed repulsive to her and she did not just "set her eyes on another man," we would compel the husband to divorce her as in the other cases in the Mishna regarding the "husbands whom we compel to divorce their wives," for similar reasons.... In this case, we happen to doubt the honesty of her statement, because we do not find in her husband those faults that she claims.... Therefore, we cannot compel the husband to divorce her; but neither dare we punish her with the loss of the monetary value of her *ketuba*. Maybe she does speak the truth, for [it is written]: "The heart knows its own bitterness."[94]

There seems to be little doubt that in cases where the rabbinical court would find a basis for the pleading of the wife, the anonymous rabbi would agree with the decision of Maimonides, and those others who think as he does, that one compels the husband to divorce his wife, because she is not his captive.

To what extent the opposition of some authorities was due to personal attitudes rather than solid halachic foundations one may judge by the following. Among those whose interpretations of the talmudic source differ from that of Maimonides is R. Isaac Alfasi. After having stated his view that according to the Talmud, in the case of the "rebellious wife" one does not compel the husband to divorce her, he continues: "This is the talmudic law. However, nowadays in the rabbinical courts of the yeshivot, this is how we rule in these cases: When a woman comes and says, 'I do not want this man; I want him to give me a *get*,' she should be given the writ of divorce immediately...." This is also reported by Rabbenu Gershon, one of the great halachic authorities of the medieval period. In the name of R. Hai Gaon, it is cited that such was the practice for over three hundred years in the Babylonian schools of the gaonic period. And yet, the great Spanish medieval commentator R. Solomon Aderet (Rashba), opposes it sharply, dismissing the gaonic practice by saying that "maybe" they meant it only as an emergency measure, a temporary arrangement that no longer has any authority behind it.

Most surprising about the attitude of Aderet is the fact that his suggestion to dismiss the gaonic practice had already been rebutted a generation earlier by Nahmanides, who is considered his teacher. Nahmanides went to the defense of Alfasi against the criticism of R. Zerachiah Halevi (known as Ba'al Hama'or), who long before Aderet also asserted that there was no gaonic practice in the matter, for the deviation from the Talmud was only a temporary measure meant for a specific time and situation. This is how Nahmanides rejected the suggestion:

> He [Alfasi] was more familiar with the rulings of the Geonim than anyone else. Undoubtedly, he means to say that they ruled for the future too. The words of the Ba'al Hama'or are another way of saying that he disagrees with the Geonim and maintains that in this matter we have to follow the talmudic law, but he says it in polite language. The truth, however, is that they introduced their ruling for generations to come. In the days of our master [i.e., Alfasi] this had been the firmly

established practice for five hundred years. This is known from their [the Geonim's] responsa.... It is also found in the works of the early as well as the later authorities. And they knew well how it was intended.

This is clear and convincing enough. Yet in conclusion Nahmanides wrote: "However, if someone wishes to be strict and not compel a husband to divorce [a 'rebellious wife'], as is the law in the Talmud, he has lost nothing; and may he be blessed."[95] One remains astounded at such words. To be "strict" in matters of divorce and overlook the happiness of the woman may often be extreme leniency in the implementation of the not-insignificant biblical commandment "And you shall love your neighbor as yourself."

In a later period other problems arose. There was the case of the husband who mistreated his wife by quarrels, anger, or beatings. The husband who repeatedly forced his wife out of the house was compelled to give her a divorce. But in the case of wife beating, one opinion is that it is a sin, and that this fact should be impressed upon the husband. One might be in greater sympathy with the other opinion, also quoted in the *Shulhan Aruch*, that if the man does not listen to "one or two warnings" by the rabbinical court, he should be compelled to divorce.[96]

We shall consider a case that is discussed in the thirteenth-century responsa of R. Samson ben Tzadok. He was asked what the law was to be for a woman whose husband caused her such continuous suffering that she despised him. "It is well known that he is a very hard man. She cannot endure him because of the continual quarrels. He also lets her starve. She has come to hate life itself." In his response, R. Samson discusses the problem from a number of angles, quoting the talmudic saying that one cannot expect anyone "to live with a snake in the same basket." Finally, he quotes the Mishna that lists the cases in which one compels a husband to divorce his wife, among them that of a man who has chronic bad breath, and concludes: "If one forces him for the odor of the mouth, how much more so for unceasing suffering that is worse than death." Most significant is the concluding comment in his responsum, which employs several talmudic sayings to make his point: "Even though I know that one finds in the works of great latter-day authorities that in such a case one does not compel the husband at all, but neither are we 'mere reed-cutters along a pond,' and in matters that depend on common sense, 'the judge has to rule by what his own eyes see.'"[97]

Problems similar to that of the "rebellious wife" take on a more serious dimension with respect to the biblical laws regarding the levirate marriage, which demanded that if a man died without leaving any children, one of his brothers had to marry his widow. Once again, we shall look at the Mishna that is introduced with the words: "And these are the husbands whom we compel to divorce their wives." We saw above that R. Meir was of the opinion that even if the woman explicitly agreed to marry the man in spite of his physical condition or profession, she might refuse to live with him after the marriage by explaining: "I thought I could endure it; now I see that I cannot." The other sages disagreed with him in this case. At the same time, the Mishna continues: "It happened that one man, a tanner, died leaving no children. He had a brother who was also a tanner. Declared the sages: In this case, the woman has the right to say: 'I was willing to accept your brother; I cannot accept you.'"

In such a case even the rabbis who disagreed with R. Meir accepted his opinion that one compels the brother-in-law to perform the *halitza* ceremony, by which the widow is freed to marry whomever she pleases.[98] But what happens when the refusal of the widow is not connected with the bodily odor of the brother-in-law inseparable from his occupation, but is of a purely personal nature, for instance, when the widow and her brother-in-law are not suited for each other? Such possibilities are discussed in the Talmud. Assuming the age difference is too great to favor a successful marriage: "If he is a mere youth and she is an old woman, or he is an old man and she a child, they say to him: 'Why would you want to marry someone so much younger than you, someone so much older than you? Go, seek someone like yourself, and do not bring quarrel into your home.'" This advice that must be given to him is based on the biblical verse: "And the elders of his city should call him and talk to him." In the case of an "unsuitable" brother-in-law, one must urge *halitza* rather than levirate marriage. In the Talmud itself there is no definition of suitability, but the following story is provided to illustrate the point: The brother-in-law wanted to marry his sister-in-law, but it was obvious that his only intention was to acquire her money. The man was tricked into freeing the widow by *halitza*. He was promised a sum of money if he performed the ceremony, and after the ceremony the wife reneged; still, the *halitza* was considered valid. Thus, in order to deal with the problem of the "unfitting" brother-in-law, the principle was laid down that a *halitza* ceremony executed under a false assumption on the part of the brother-in-law is nevertheless valid.[99]

This was, however, only a partial solution to the problem. What was to be done if the unfitting brother-in-law did not allow himself to be misled? The question was attacked more fundamentally with the case of the widow who refused to marry her brother-in-law, not because of any shortcoming of his, but simply because she had no desire to marry him. This is not the place to present the entire discussion of the subject by the halachic authorities. Needless to say, all those authorities who ruled that the woman who refused to continue a marriage must be given the desired divorce would also rule that the brother-in-law must submit to *halitza*. But even the halachic authorities who would not allow an enforced divorce in the case of a marriage are inclined toward leniency in order to free a widow from her levirate bonds.

Among the authorities who disagreed with Maimonides' ruling in the case of the "rebellious wife" was R. Asher ben Yehiel (Rosh), who lived in Germany and Spain in the late thirteenth and early fourteenth centuries. Yet in the case of a brother-in-law whom the widow refused to marry because he was young and ignorant, he ruled that one compels the brother-in-law to agree to *halitza*.[100] Once again it was R. Samson ben Tzadok who asserted that if the widow, for reasons of her own, refuses to marry her brother-in-law, he has to be forced to free her through the *halitza* ceremony. He fortified his decision with the statement that even those who disagree with Maimonides' opinion in the case of the "rebellious wife" respect the plea of the widow to be freed by compelling the brother-in-law in this case. His argument was that "the teachers in the Talmud were stricter in matters of divorce than in those of *halitza*." Actually there is a clear talmudic statement that one "must not suppress the pleas of the widow" (i.e., who refuses to marry a brother-in-law).[101] While this may be understood in various ways, the interpretation that the widow has the right to refuse to enter into the levirate marriage is accepted by the classical commentator of the Talmud, Rashi, and is expressed in one of the earliest and most authoritative halachic codes, the ninth-century *Halachot Gedolot*.

A number of other innovative regulations were introduced by the talmudic teachers in order to remedy the legally weak status of the married woman. One of their major concerns in this regard was to protect the wife against becoming an *aguna*, a woman whose husband for whatever reason cannot be reached for purposes of a divorce. She is legally married, but she has no husband and yet cannot remarry. (The Hebrew word *ogen* means "anchor"; the woman is "anchored," tied to a situation from which there seems to be no release.)

Various laws that generally apply were declared inoperative in divorce proceedings in order to reduce the likelihood of a woman becoming an *aguna*. For instance, a messenger who brought a writ of divorce, or *get*, sent by a husband to his wife, from Babylon to the land of Israel, had to testify that the divorce document was written as required by the Torah, "in his name and in her name and for the purpose of divorce." (According to the law, if a *get* is written on behalf of one man to divorce his wife, and after its completion it is handed to another man whose name and whose wife's name are identical with those that appear in the document, it is invalid; so is a *get* written for the sake of writing practice.) Normally, two witnesses are required to testify. In this case, however, it was ruled that the testimony of the messenger alone was sufficient. The reason for this had to

do with the conditions of the time. There were not many travelers between Babylon and the land of Israel. Had one insisted on
two witnesses, considerable delays might have occurred in the
sending of a writ of divorce; in numerous cases, the writ would
never have been sent, and the woman would have become an
aguna. In order to prevent this from happening, "the rabbis were
lenient."[102]

Another example: A *get* required the signatures of two witnesses. Assuming now that the witnesses who were available
could not sign their names, what was to be done? The decision
was that the signatures were prefigured in the document in such
a manner that the witnesses had only to fill in the ink. This was
the only document where such a practice was permissible. Said
R. Elazar: "This was done so that the daughters of Israel not
become *agunot*."[103]

In this case the deviation from the norm was not from biblical but only from rabbinical laws: Since the majority of the
Babylonian scribes were familiar with the rules of writing *gitin*,
the demand for testimony was only a rabbinical requirement.
Similarly, the filling in of a prefigured signature by a witness was
not against biblical law. However, we find that even when the
problem presented concerned a biblical injunction, the rabbis
found a way, outside the generally valid norm, to save a woman
from the status of an *aguna*. This was the case of the wife whose
husband went to "a land beyond the sea," a faraway country
with which there was no possibility of normal communication.
One witness arrived from that land and testified that the man
had died. According to the Bible, facts are to be established in
court on the strength of the testimony of two witnesses. Nevertheless, the rabbis of the Talmud allowed the woman to remarry.

They went even further. According to biblical law, one may testify only from direct personal knowledge, but not on the basis of knowledge learned from another person's testimony. Neither is the testimony of a woman or a slave admitted. But in this case, it was ruled not only that the testimony of one witness was sufficient, but that the witness may testify on the basis of hearsay, and that the witness may be a woman or even a slave.

Why was all this permitted? The Talmud explains it as follows: Should the husband still be alive and eventually return after his wife's remarriage, the consequences for her would be extremely serious, for even though she was still married, she had entered into another, illegal marriage. According to the law, she would have to leave her second "husband," but she could not return to her original husband. She would be adjudged an adulteress. Her children by her second, legally invalid marriage would be considered illegitimate. She would also have forfeited any compensation due her from the first marriage contract in case of divorce. Because of the very serious consequences of mistaken testimony, it was assumed that the woman would be most careful. Before entering into another marriage, she would consider the entire situation, investigate herself, and make sure that the testimony was reliable. "Because of the dire consequences [in case of error] at the end, one was lenient at the beginning." The final words in the discussion of the subject are: "Because of the danger of her becoming an *aguna*, one made it easier for her."[104]

One of the boldest halachic innovations was the annulment of marriage in certain situations. Since a divorce could be effected only by the husband handing a *get* to his wife, the husband also had the power to cancel the writ of divorce before it reached her. He could send the document by a messenger, and before the messenger had time to deliver it, the husband could appear before a rabbinical court and declare that he had invalidated the writ, in which case the divorce did not take place. Without a writ there could be no divorce, and this *get*, having been canceled, became a mere piece of paper. Legally, the husband could cancel the validity of the divorce document even without notifying his wife or his messenger. This could lead to the unfortunate situation of a woman receiving such a document and believing that she was now divorced. If she then entered into a new marriage, she had technically committed adultery, with all the disastrous consequences involved. In order to remedy the situation, R. Gamliel the Elder, who lived in the first century c.e. and was one of the most respected heads of the Sanhedrin, instituted an ordinance "that one should not cancel a *get* in the absence of his messenger or his wife," that is, without their knowledge. One should not do it "for the sake of the correction of the world" (*tikun olam*).

But what happened if a person disregarded the edict of R. Gamliel the Elder? A later generation of mishnaic teachers, R. Yehuda Hanasi and his son R. Gamliel, debated the issue. Both were descendants of R. Gamliel the Elder. R. Yehuda Hanasi was of the opinion that if a husband, defying the ordinance of R. Gamliel the Elder, did cancel a writ of divorce, the document became invalid. For indeed, according to biblical law, the husband does have that right. His son R. Gamliel, however, ruled that after the edict of R. Gamliel the Elder any cancellation of a *get* without the knowledge of the wife or the messenger is ineffective. The writ remains valid, and the divorce does take place. "Otherwise," he argued, "of what worth is the authority of the court of law?" A powerful attack was mounted in the Talmud against his view: "Is there such a thing as a divorce that is invalid according to biblical law, and merely because 'of what worth is the authority of the court of law?' we free a married woman to marry whomever she pleases?" The Talmud's answer: "Indeed so: He who marries a woman does so with the understanding that the legal basis of the marriage is the law as perceived by the rabbis [Rashi's explanation: In the formula the groom says to the bride, 'You are sanctified to me in accordance with the law of Moses and Israel']. They retroactively annulled this marriage."[105]

The principle of the annulment of marriage is applied in the Talmud in a number of different situations. Earlier we discussed the ruling of Rava that in matters of divorce, the generally valid principle of *ones rahmana patrei*—that a person is not responsible for an action that takes place due to unexpected circumstances beyond his control—was inoperative. Accordingly, he ruled that a divorce given with the condition that it should take effect only if the husband did not return after a specified absence is valid, and the woman is considered duly divorced, even if the husband desired to return but was prevented from doing so by the unforeseen intervention of some superior force or circumstance. His reason was twofold. First, the loyal wives would become *agunot*, for even when a husband refused to return, they would assume that he was prevented from doing so against his will and would thus consider themselves still married. Second, the less loyal wives, on the contrary, would only too easily conclude that the husband intentionally did not return and would consider themselves divorced, even though the husband was prevented from returning because of unexpected circumstances and, therefore, they were really not divorced. Here, too, the question was raised: According to the biblically valid principle of *ones*, that writ was not valid and, therefore, there was no divorce. Rava, because of his personal consideration of the possible consequences of a biblical law, nonetheless declared women who are married according to biblical law to be divorced. Again, the act was justified by reasoning that since all marriages are concluded on the basis of the halacha as understood by the rabbis, they also have the authority to annul them retroactively.[106]

An even more striking example of the function of this principle may be understood from the following example: According to biblical law, a father can arrange a marriage for a daughter who is a minor. (We saw earlier that already in the second century the rabbis in the Talmud attempted to curb this in practice.) The death of the father could cause serious social problems. In such a case, often there was no one to look after the minor. The rabbis of the Talmud decreed that the mother or the brothers of the minor could also conclude a marriage on her behalf. However, such a marriage was a rabbinical one; it had no biblical basis. According to biblical law, the young girl was not married to the husband to whom she had been given in marriage by her family. According to one opinion, when such a child-wife came of age, another marriage ceremony had to be performed. In the discussion of this theme the story is told: Once, when such a child came of age, the "husband" led her to the marriage canopy in order to marry her again in accordance with biblical law. As they were preparing for the ceremony, another man came, grabbed the bride, escaped with her, and formally married her.

In this case, according to biblical law she was married to the second man. Yet the talmudic teachers invalidated this marriage. To the question of how they could annul a marriage concluded in accordance with biblical law, the answer is given: "He acted improperly, so they dealt with him 'improperly' and annulled his marriage." Once again explains Rashi: Since marriages are concluded in accordance with the rules of the rabbis, they have the authority to invalidate a marriage concluded by improper means.[107]

It is quite obvious that the rabbis were fully aware of the legally disadvantaged status of the woman. They were disturbed by it and endeavored to correct the situation through innovative rulings and rabbinical regulations. The process continued for centuries after the conclusion of the Talmud in the fifth century. Among the best-known post-talmudic regulations are the tenth-century bans of Rabbenu Gershon against polygamy (a ruling foreshadowed already in the Talmud) and against the husband who divorces his wife against her will. The ban of Rabbenu Gershon implied the exclusion of the violator from the community. R. Asher ben Yehiel, father of the author of the *Arba'a Turim*, the code upon which the structure of R. Joseph Karo's *Shulhan Aruch* was based, in one of his responsa remarked that the purpose of Rabbenu Gershon in requiring the wife's consent to a divorce was "to equalize the power of the woman to that of the man: As he divorces only by his free will, so can she not be divorced either except if she freely agrees to a divorce."[108]

CHAPTER TWO

The Nature of Halachic Authority

"NOT IN HEAVEN"

The Torah was given at Sinai. It was given to a whole nation as a way of life for all generations. However, in order to guide the daily life of an entire people through all its history, not only knowledge of the Torah is needed. A leadership is required to deal with the problems of the day as they arise—with questions of interpretation—and it must have the authority to make decisions. The seat of that leadership and authority was the Sanhedrin, the Supreme Court of seventy-one sages in Jerusalem. The institution continued to exist on the basis of voluntary acceptance by the Jewish people for several generations after the destruction of the Second Commonwealth. When it ceased to function, leadership and authority passed on to the scholars in the various communities in the countries of the Jewish people's dispersion. They interpreted the meaning of the Torah and tradition and taught them in the talmudic academies.

The nature of the authority of the scholars found its boldest expression in a story told in the Talmud and known as the discussion around the *tanur shel Aknai*, the "Aknai oven." The subject matter was a question of ritual purity. There was sharp disagreement between the majority of the sages and the mighty R. Eliezer, who—so it would seem from the context—surpassed them all. Upon the call of R. Eliezer, a number of miracles occurred as signs that his opinion was the correct one. His colleagues were not impressed. Finally, a heavenly voice was heard: "What is it you want with R. Eliezer? Wherever he expresses an opinion, the halacha is according to him." This would seem to have settled the issue; but not for the rabbis. Upon hearing the heavenly voice, R. Yehoshua stood up and, in response, called out: "It is not in the heaven." The words were interpreted in the Talmud as meaning: "The Torah has already been given to us at Sinai. We are not to listen to a heavenly voice [i.e., in matters of halachic decision]. For you have already written for us at Sinai to make decisions in accordance with the opinion of the majority." The story has a charming postscript. R. Natan once encountered the prophet Elijah (who, according to the biblical story, never died, but ascended to heaven and according to popular belief occasionally roams in this world) and asked him: "What was God doing at the time of that great discussion?" Elijah's reply was: "God was laughing and said: 'My sons have defeated me; my sons have defeated me.'"[1]

It would seem to us that this story has twofold significance. First of all, there is an insistence on the human share and responsibility in the interpretation and administration of the revealed word of God. Since the Torah had been given to human beings, it could not be otherwise. It was inconceivable that every time a question arose or a problem presented itself, one should have to contact the heavenly authority for a decision. God himself, in the act of revelation, handed the deciding authority to man.

Of no less importance is the second aspect of this story. Whose opinion was the correct one: that of R. Eliezer or that of the majority of the sages? In an absolute sense, R. Eliezer was, of course, right. The very heavens agreed with him. However, the affairs of men cannot be guided by absolute objectivity, only by human objectivity. What God desires of the Jewish people is that it live by his word in accordance with its own understanding. In theoretical discussions man strives to delve into the ultimate depth of the truth, but when he decides he has reached it, it is still only his own human insight that affirms that indeed he has found it. When it is necessary to make decisions about human conduct and behavior, one can do so only on the basis of pragmatic principles; for example, "follow the view of the majority." The result is not objective truth but pragmatic validity. For this reason, the majority of the rabbis was right and the great R. Eliezer, supported by a heavenly voice of absolute truth, was wrong.[2]

The same insight emerges from a confrontation between R. Gamliel and R. Yehoshua, who so courageously silenced the heavenly voice in the preceding story. The argument between them revolved around the evaluation of the testimony of witnesses who testified to having seen the new moon. R. Yehoshua adjudged their testimony unreliable. His calculation of the calendar therefore differed from that of R. Gamliel, who was the head of the Sanhedrin. To halt any further discussion of the matter, R. Gamliel ordered R. Yehoshua to appear before him "with his staff and haversack" on the day that would be Yom Kippur, the Day of Atonement, according to R. Yehoshua's ruling. In other words, he ordered him to treat that day as a weekday. R. Yehoshua obeyed the order. As in the preceding account, no decision was made here on the objective truth of either opinion. On the basis of the interpretation of the relevant biblical passage, R. Akiva explained that the determination of the dates of the festival is completely in the hands of the Sanhedrin, even if it should be mistaken in its calculations.³ There is no other way of establishing an ordered calendar sequence in the life of a nation. Objectively, R. Yehoshua might have been right in rejecting the testimony of the witnesses, but for pragmatic reasons the halacha was according to R. Gamliel, the head of the Sanhedrin. The treatment meted out to R. Eliezer was also the lot of R. Yehoshua.

It is important to note that precisely because the authoritative opinion of the Sanhedrin or of the majority in any rabbinical court possesses only pragmatic truth, the objective value of the minority view is not eliminated. In both stories we have discussed, this is apparent in the behavior of the "victor" toward the colleague whose position was rejected. The *herem*, the ban of social ostracism, was pronounced over R. Eliezer because of his behavior, not because of his opinion in the matter. His colleagues were concerned to communicate it to him without hurting him more than was absolutely necessary. Once again it was R. Akiva who took the task upon himself. He clothed himself in black garments (as a sign of his personal grief) and went to R. Eliezer. He sat down before him at a distance of four cubits (as was the rule with a person in *herem*). When R. Eliezer asked for an explanation, he said: "Master! It seems to me that your colleagues have separated themselves from you."⁴ Very similar was the behavior of R. Gamliel toward R. Yehoshua. When R. Yehoshua appeared before him as ordered on the day that was Yom Kippur according to R. Yehoshua's calculation, "R. Gamliel stood up, kissed him on the head, and said to him: 'Come in peace, my teacher and disciple: my teacher in wisdom, my disciple in that you obeyed my words.'"[5]

Because one often had to be satisfied with the pragmatic validity of the final halachic decision, one treated with respect the holder of the defeated minority teaching. Not only was he treated with respect as an individual, but so were their teachings. Earlier we had occasion to quote a mishna which stated that the minority opinions have been preserved so that if a rabbinical court ever arises that finds the rejected view of an individual teacher justified, it will have the authority to accept it and to rule accordingly against a previously followed practice established in accordance with the majority.[6] The minority view is kept in abeyance; it has been overruled conditionally, till such time as valid arguments might be found for its acceptance. The teaching of the minority is not suppressed; it retains its theoretical validity.

One may find a further realization of this idea in the case of the *zaken mamre*, the "rebellious elder," who disregards the decision of the Sanhedrin. Here is how Maimonides, basing himself completely on the talmudic text, describes the procedure that led to this rebel's punishment:

> How is the *zaken mamre* judged? If a sage, who has the authority to render decisions, rules on a matter that has been in doubt... [and his ruling is not accepted by other sages], he and those who disagree with him go up to Jerusalem and appear before the *beit din* (rabbinical court) that sits at the gate of the Temple Mount. That court tells them what the law is. If he [the rebellious elder] accepts it, good.

If not, they all approach the *beit din* at the door of the Temple court. They too tell him what the law is. If he accepts it, good. If not, they all have to go to the High Court [i.e., the Sanhedrin] that sits in the "Chamber of the Hewn Stone," whence Torah goes forth to all Israel.... This court tells them, "Such is the law." After that they all leave. If this sage, returning to his city, continues to learn and to teach as before, he is free. If he instructs the people to act according to his own teaching, or if he himself acts in that manner, he is subject to capital punishment.[7]

Decisions of the High Court in Jerusalem were the law of the land. If one of the elders, who himself was a teacher and judge in his own city, defied them (in certain more serious matters), he was guilty. His punishment was death if he broke the law by his own action or taught others to do so, but he was free to continue to teach and propagate his own views which were contrary to the decisions of the High Court. The pragmatic validity of the Sanhedrin's decision did not rule out the possible truth value of an opposing view, which one day may yet become the accepted halacha.

"THESE AS WELL AS THOSE ARE WORDS OF THE LIVING GOD"

We have learned that in cases of disagreement between the masters of the halacha, there is often no way of deciding which is the logically true opinion. The decision in such cases is based on pragmatic considerations. Therefore, the opinion of the minority is not suppressed; indeed, its time, too, may come one day. The question that may be raised is: How can halachic decisions always be considered the rule of the Torah and not the subjective opinions of its teachers? It would seem to us that the Talmud was fully aware of this problem and provided an ingenious solution for it. One of the great mishnaic teachers, R. Elazar ben Azarya, expressed it in a midrashic interpretation of a verse in Ecclesiastes. Toward the end of his sayings, Kohelet evaluates "the words of the wise." He compares them to some objects that are "composed in collections." "They [i.e., the words of the wise] are given from one shepherd." The Hebrew words that are rendered as "composed in collections" call forth an association with "composed by men of assemblies." Hence the following interpretation:

> "Men of assemblies" are *talmidei hachamim* [disciples of the wise; i.e., talmudic scholars] who sit in their assemblies and occupy themselves with the Torah. Some rule: defiled; others, purify; some forbid, others permit; some reject, others accept. Should one say: "How then can I learn now?" That is why it is also written: "They are given from one shepherd." One God gave them all. One teacher [i.e., Moses] spoke them according to the words of the Master of all the words, blessed be he. As it is written: "and God spoke all these words." So listen with great attention and seek to acquire an understanding heart to grasp the words of those who defile as well as of those who purify; of those who forbid as well as of those who permit; of those who reject as well as of those who accept.[8]

The Torah was given to the people of Israel. It obligates the Jew to study it and to seek to understand it; it demands of the sages of Israel that they interpret it and teach it as guidance and law for everyday living. Since the Torah was given not to angels but to human beings, and since it depends on interpretation and understanding by human beings, whatever is discovered in it by human beings who accept the Torah as God's revelation to the Jewish people at Sinai and study it is indeed the truth of the Torah. That is how the sages of Israel understood what happened at the time of God's revelation at Sinai. The psalmist says of the event that the voice of God sounded "with might." The psalmist does not say, "With his might." No human being could have survived it. The people received the voice; young and old, men, women, and children, each according to his own strength.[9] Human beings receive even the revelation of God only with their human capacities. Once a Jew accepts the Torah from Sinai, whatever it teaches him in his search for its meaning and message is the word of God for him. The giver of the Torah to mere man accepts responsibility for it; it is Torah. Of the great discussions and sharp disagreements between the schools of Shamai and Hillel, a voice from heaven was heard to proclaim: "These as well as those are words of the living God."[10] The subjective human element is not to be eliminated from the acceptance of the Torah. It was included in the meaning of the Torah from the very beginning. Needless to say, there have to be principles by which to determine the halacha, the law for the people to live by.

According to one opinion in the Jerusalem Talmud, the human share in the interpretation of the Torah is unavoidable; it is vital for the realization of the Torah in the life of the people through its changing history.

R. Yanai said: Had the Torah been given as one cut [i.e., as
one final, unchangeable decision in all matters without any
possibility of divergent interpretations; see commentaries on
the text], we could not stand on our feet. "And God spoke to
Moses" [i.e., he gave him the Torah]—At that time, Moses
said to him: "Make known to me how the halacha is to be
decided." He answered him: "One has to accept the opinion
of the majority. If the majority acquits, acquit him; if it finds
him guilty, punish. The Torah must be capable of forty-nine
ways of interpretation affirming an opinion and forty-nine
ways opposing it." [We render the meaning here, not a literal translation.][11]

Why, indeed, was it necessary to formulate the text of the
Torah in such a manner that it be open to so many possibilities
of interpretation? It would seem to us that in saying that Moses
was asking God to tell him the final halacha, R. Yanai intends to
tell us that it is not for man to ask of God that he reveal to him
the ultimate, objective truth; it is not for us to ask for the "voice
from heaven" to pronounce the halachic decision as a dictate
from on high for all generations. That is impossible, for in such
a case one could not live with such a Torah. One commentator
on the Jerusalem Talmud explains: "The world could not exist; it
must be possible to interpret the Torah this way and that way...
'and these as well as those are the words of the living God.'" It is
a pity that our commentator did not fully say why this was necessary and why the world could not stand otherwise.

One gains further insight into R. Yanai's statement from
what the Jewish sages of thirteenth-century France had to say on
this subject. The question before them was: How is it possible

that when "one permits" and "the other forbids," both should be speaking words of the living God? Their answer:

> When Moses ascended on high to receive the Torah, they showed him in every case forty-nine possibilities "of forbidding" and forty-nine possibilities "of permitting." He asked the Holy One, blessed be he, about it. He was answered that the intention was that all these possibilities of interpretation should be entrusted to the sages of Israel of each generation, that the decision be in accordance with their resolution.[12]

These French sages seem to sum up the sayings of R. Elazar ben Azarya and R. Yanai. They add, however, that the various possibilities of interpretation and halachic decision were left to the teachers of each generation. In other words, interpretations that "forbid" and are accepted in one generation may be supplanted by interpretations that "permit" in another. Both are the words of the living God, for the Torah, from its inception, takes notice of the needs of the hour, acknowledging changes in the material as well as the spiritual history of the people. Without it, as R. Yanai maintains, we would have "no foot on which to stand."

We may add here Rashi's interpretation of that remarkable phrase, "these as well as those are the words of the living God":

> When two rabbis of the Talmud disagree with each other about the law... there is no untruth there. Each of them justifies his opinion. One gives a reason to permit, the other, reason to forbid. One compares the case before him to one precedent; the other compares it to something different. It is possible to say, "Both speak the words of the living God."

> At times, one reason is valid; at other times, another reason. For reasons change even in the wake of only slight changes in the situation.[13]

This clarifies further the words of the French sages. All "forty-nine possibilities" are the "words of the living God." Each variant may have its day; as the result of even only "slight changes," it may become the accepted halacha for its hour.

"only what the judge's eyes see"

This heading is an inexact rendering of a quotation from the Talmud. A more literal translation would be: "A judge must be guided only by what his own eyes see." However, even that requires some clarification before we may enter into a discussion of its significance. First, one should understand that the word "judge" is used here not in the limited, technical sense in which the word is used in English. In the talmudic context, it stands for a sage who is a teacher of the Torah in its comprehensive totality and is authorized to rule on all matters concerning the life of the individual and society, be they of a civic-social or a purely ritual nature, regarding commandments between man and his fellow or between man and God. To avoid misunderstandings, from here on we shall use the Hebrew term *dayan*, which is used in the original.

The phrase "by what he sees with his own eyes" must also not be taken literally. It does not mean a *dayan* has to witness the situation about which he pronounces his decision. "What he sees" stands for "what he understands by his own insight and reason." Whenever a *dayan* has to make a decision, he must follow his own understanding. This is, indeed, one of the basic principles of halachic authority. No other principle expresses more succinctly the human share in the application of Torah to an actual life situation.

The principle has a twofold meaning:

In one passage in the Talmud, it is used to encourage the sages to accept the responsibility of making decisions. "A *dayan* might say: 'What do I need all this anguish for [i.e., the doubts that I might err in my decision]?' To him the Bible says: 'He is with you in giving judgment.' A *dayan* should be guided only by his own understanding [of the case before him]."[14] Nothing more is required of him than that he judge the case to the best of his knowledge and understanding. From a story in the Talmud about R. Yehuda Hanasi, one learns that once the *dayan* has reached a decision, he must not change it merely out of fear that he might have been wrong. Should he do that, he would certainly be wrong, for a *dayan* must follow his own understanding and not his fears.[15]

Another meaning of this principle emerges from a conversation that Rava had with his disciples. The disciples were occupied with the question of how to deal with halachic decisions by their master that they found difficult to accept. As long as Rava was alive, the problem was not too serious. They could always ask him for elucidation. But what was to be their attitude toward the rulings of their master after his death? Rava gave them this advice: "After my death, you should not tear them up. For if I were alive, I might explain to you my reasons. But neither should you accept them, for a *dayan* should be guided only by his own understanding."[16]

The great significance of this discussion lies in the fact that the principle of the acceptance of personal responsibility applies not only in cases in which no previous decisions are extant; even when decisions have already been given by a master and teacher, his disciples after him may overrule him. Two classical commentators on the Talmud give their own interpretations. Rashbam (who fills in for Rashi where that commentary is not available) simply says that Rava meant that his disciples should not be guided by his decisions, because it was the responsibility of the *dayan* to rule according to his own insight. More original is the interpretation of Rabbenu Gershon. He understood Rava's quoting of the principle of personal decision responsibility as a reference to Rava's own decisions that might be questioned by his students: "As if to say [regarding those decisions]: 'I made those decisions as the matter appeared to me then. Maybe at another time I would have seen it differently.'"[17]

There is no real difference between the two interpretations. But whereas Rashbam simply states that disciples may overrule their master after his death because of their responsibility to make decisions to the best of their grasp of the issues before them, Rabbenu Gershon seems to explain why this should be so. According to him, Rava was saying that after his death, his decisions ought not to have any authority for his disciples merely because of their respect for him. Since the *dayan* rules according to his personal understanding, there is always a subjective element attached to his decisions. They are, therefore, conditioned by personality, time, and place. They have no automatic authority beyond his own life, for perhaps he himself, had he lived longer, or at a different time, would have seen things differently and would also have ruled differently.

Two halachic authorities summed up the personal aspect of the responsibility of the *dayan* in highly significant formulations. R. Abraham the son of Maimonides put it this way in one of his responsa:

> The rule in the matter is—say I—that a *dayan* who in his decisions follows only what is written and clearly stated is weak and wanting. Such an attitude invalidates what they [i.e., our sages] said: "A *dayan* should be guided only by his own understanding." [With him] it is not so. What is written are the roots. Every *dayan* and everyone who renders decisions must weigh them according to each case that comes before him. Every decision [that he is considering] he should compare to something similar to it. He should develop branches from the roots. The numerous case histories in the Talmud, which incorporate only part of the laws, were not reported for nothing; but neither were they recorded so that in those matters the law should always be as it is written there. They were preserved only so the wise man, by hearing them often, should acquire efficiency in weighing matters rationally, as well as a good method of making decisions.[18]

Even more pronounced on this subject are the words of the author of the *Ketzot Hahoshen*. This is what he teaches us in the introduction to his commentary on *Hoshen Hamishpat*:

> One trembles at the thought that one might say about the Torah things that are not true, i.e., that the human mind is too weak to grasp the truth.... The Torah was not given to ministering angels. It was given to man with a human mind.

He gave us the Torah in conformity to the ability of the
human mind to decide, even though it may not be the truth
[i.e., objectively speaking]... only true according to the con-
clusions of the human mind.... Let the truth emerge from
the earth. The truth be as the sages decide with the human
mind.

This seems to be the boldest formulation of R. Yehoshua's
exclamation: "It is not in heaven!" Halacha, as the human way
of life in accordance with the Torah, does not aim at absolute
truth, nor does it run after the *fata morgana* of universal truth.
Neither of them is accessible to human beings. Its aim is "earthly
truth" that the human intellect can grasp and for whose pursu-
ance in life man must accept personal responsibility.

To conclude what has been said thus far on the subject of
this chapter, it seems necessary to say a few words on the significance of the halachic principle that one court may not abrogate
the words of a "fellow court," unless it is greater in wisdom and
numbers than the other (the majority principle at work).[19]

First, we have learned that the variants of Torah interpretation have been handed over to the sages of each age to decide
the halacha according to their understanding. We have found
the strong insistence on the principle that the *dayan* has to make
his decision as he himself sees the case before him. Discussion
of this aspect of our theme would be halachically too technical to fit into this presentation.[20] It is important to realize the
contemporaneous nature of halachic decisions. They deal with
the situation at hand. This does not mean abrogating a previous
decision of a respected halachic authority. It requires the legitimate application of halachic principles to the concrete situation
of the hour, with which the preceding court did not deal.

Let us once again consider the *prozbul*, introduced by Hillel so that private debts should not be canceled at the approach of the sabbatical year. This is one example of a *takana* (a new regulation) that only a court superior to that of Hillel could abolish. Assuming, however, that an economic situation may yet arise in which the proper functioning of the credit system may coexist with the literal observance of the biblical sabbatical law, surely abolishing the use of the *prozbul* would not mean overruling the great Hillel. Let us recall the words of Rava to his disciples—that after his death, they should not be guided by his decisions, for at a later time he himself might have changed his mind. The key phrase in the principle quoted is "the words of *a fellow court*." "A fellow court" is a contemporaneous one, not in the chronological sense, but in terms of the continued identity of the situation, the nature of the problem, and the needs and ethical quality of the individual and society.[21]

Second, the principle is mentioned only in the establishment of the binding quality of *takanot* and *gezerot*, remedial regulations (like the *prozbul*) or restrictive ones (such as *stam yeinan*). It is never used to strengthen the authority of actual Torah interpretation or halachic decision by a superior authority. On the contrary, in the preceding paragraph in which Maimonides notes the authority of *takanot* and *gezerot*, he has the following to say:[22]

Regarding a court that interpreted according to one of the rules [of Torah interpretation] as it appeared right in their eyes, if after them another court arose to which another argument appeared to be right, to abolish that of the previous one, it abolishes that argument and it rules as it deems correct. For it is written: "to the judge who will be in those days"; you are obligated only to go to the court of your generation.

This statement by Maimonides is based on the Talmud.[23]

To illustrate the point with a case history, we return to the responsum of the Tashbatz, R. Samson ben Tzadok, that we discussed earlier in another context. It concerned the case of a woman who suffered a great deal from the treatment she received from her husband. The author elaborates on why, in this case, one should compel the husband to divorce her. He concludes: "Although it is known to me that it is found in the responsa of the great latter-day scholars that in cases of this nature one does not compel the husband... in matters that depend on logical reasoning the *dayan* must decide as he himself sees it."[24] No matter what the preceding authorities had decided, *this* woman never came before them with her suffering—on *this* case they had never ruled. If the *dayan* had valid reasons, he was the authority to rule according to his own insights and after giving due consideration to even greater authorities who lived before him.

"UPROOTING" BIBLICAL COMMANDMENTS?

The word "uprooting" in connection with biblical commandments might be surprising to one unfamiliar with halacha. However, the subject is actually discussed in the Talmud. One of the teachers in the Talmud, R. Hisda, is indeed of the opinion that the sages (i.e., the qualified teachers of halacha) have the authority to uproot even a biblical law. Of course, there must be some valid reason to do so.

Let us illustrate by an example with which we are already familiar: the *takana* (ordinance) of R. Gamliel the Elder that a man who divorces his wife through a messenger should not annul the *get* while the messenger is on the way, without the messenger's or the wife's knowledge. The question arose: What if the husband violates this *takana* and annuls the divorce document before it reaches his wife? As we saw, a later descendant of R. Gamliel the Elder, R. Shimon ben Gamliel, declared that the husband's annulment has no effect; the *get* is valid, and the wife is divorced.[25]

Here we have, then, an example of a rabbinical ordinance's uprooting a biblical law. According to biblical law, as long as the wife never came into possession of the divorce document, the husband may change his mind and declare it invalid. Consequently, she is not divorced. In this case, however, the rabbis maintain the validity of the *get* against the biblical rule, and a married woman is declared divorced. In this instance, the generality of the law could lead to morally unacceptable consequences. The area within which the law was functioning was therefore fenced in by rabbinical decree. Indeed, the attempt is made to prove R. Hisda right that the sages have the authority "to uproot something from the Torah." The proof is rejected with the argument that since all marriages by Jews are concluded with the understanding that their legality be determined in accordance with the laws of Moses and Israel, should the husband break any of them, even if they were instituted by the rabbis, the marriage itself is annulled retroactively.[26]

In the Babylonian Talmud, the final result of the discussion between R. Hisda and his adversary, R. Natan, is a form of compromise. R. Natan agrees with R. Hisda that the sages may limit the applicability of a biblical commandment, but only by way of omission, not by way of commission.[27] For instance, it is a biblical commandment to blow the *shofar* (the ram's horn) on Rosh Hashana, the festival of the New Year. However, when Rosh Hashana falls on the Sabbath, the rabbis forbid the blowing of the *shofar*. Since the art of blowing the *shofar* correctly in accordance with the rules has to be learned, it might happen that in some small community or congregation, one would have to go and look for someone to teach him the art of *shofar*-blowing on Rosh Hashana itself. The person going to learn might take a *shofar* along with him, but should this be on the Sabbath, it would lead to the desecration of a holy day, since one must not carry any object on the Sabbath. To avoid this desecration, it was ruled that there be no blowing of the *shofar* when Rosh Hashana occurs on the Sabbath. This is an instance of "uprooting" a divine commandment by omission. But the validating of a divorce that is invalid according to the Torah, and allowing the woman to remarry, would be "uprooting" by commission.

This, however, is by far not the last word on the subject. In another context we have discussed the rabbinical innovation as regards the admissibility of certain testimonies, normally not accepted, in order to protect a woman from becoming an *aguna*.[28] To accept the testimony of only one witness, or to allow a woman, a slave, etc., to testify to the death of a husband goes against the biblical law which prescribes that the truth of any fact has to be established by two male witnesses who are not slaves. One might be satisfied with the reason given in the Talmud for this exception: "since otherwise the woman might become an *aguna* [one married yet without a husband], the rabbis exercised leniency." It would be a typical case of halachic authorities' limiting the general validity of a law because of its unacceptable consequences in a specific situation.

For the talmudic commentators, however, such an explanation seemed implausible. They wondered why R. Hisda did not prove his point by making use of this mishnaic teaching about testimony in the case of the husband who left his wife and cannot be reached. In the debate in the Talmud, he cites a number of sources to buttress his position; they are all rejected as inconclusive. But here, there seems to be irrefutable evidence for the correctness of his point of view, and yet no one makes mention of it.[29] They assumed, therefore, that the leniency in order to protect the woman from becoming an *aguna* must have a different explanation. In searching for it, the commentators and codifiers came up with some most original ideas. We shall begin with the interpretation of Maimonides:

> Let it not appear to you difficult [to understand] that the sages freed a married woman (*ha'erva hahamura*) by such testimony... the Torah insists on two witnesses and on the other laws regarding witnesses only when there is no other way of clarifying a matter except by the mouth of witnesses and their counsel; for instance, when they testify that one person killed another or borrowed money from him. But in a case whose truth may be ascertained without relying exclusively on the mouth of the witness—for instance, when he would not be able to exculpate himself should his testimony be proved untrue, as when he testifies that someone died— the Torah does not insist [that he not be relied upon]. In such a case, it is most unlikely that the witness would testify

falsely. Therefore, the sages were lenient... so that the daughters of Israel may not become *agunot*.[30]

Maimonides makes a twofold statement here. First, he advises us that even though the Torah says: "by the mouth of two witnesses or by the mouth of three witnesses shall a matter be established,"[31] this is not to be understood as a *conditio sine qua non*. The Torah means that this is how it should be done if there is no other way of determining the truth. However, where other means are available, a court is free to use them. Second, while the testimonies admitted in order to free a woman from bondage to an ever-absent husband may not be fully reliable, they are most unlikely to be false. Therefore, in order that the daughters of Israel not become *agunot*, the halachic teachers were lenient. They accepted witnesses who otherwise would not be relied upon.

Even more far-reaching is an interpretation that Ritva, R. Yomtov ben Avraham Asvili, quotes in the name of his teacher and praises highly. He writes:

It was acknowledged by the sages that because of the very serious consequences for the woman should the testimony prove false [if she got remarried, she would be entering into marriage with a second man while still married to her first husband], this is a matter whose truth or falsehood is bound to be revealed ultimately. [The idea is that the woman would make very thorough inquiries herself.][32] Therefore, it is certain that the testimony is true. Since she is extremely careful before deciding on a new marriage, she marries lawfully, and we [the court] are witness to the fact. The public knowledge that accompanies a case of this nature is to be considered complete testimony, even according to biblical law. The Torah entrusted it to the discretion of the sages to decide when public knowledge of a testimony is adequate indication of its truth....[33]

This explanation goes much further than that of Maimonides. Like Maimonides, Ritva affirms that two witnesses are not always essential. But whereas for Maimonides the "publicity" surrounding the case renders the reliability of the witness only very likely (and, therefore, leniency was exercised by the rabbis), in the view of Ritva this testimony is certainly true and has the strength of biblically approved testimony.[34]

An even more original interpretation is found in the Tosafot. They reject the idea that because of the circumstances the court itself attests to the truth of the testimony and, therefore, that this witness is acceptable even according to biblical requirements. Yet he is admitted and relied upon on the basis of a rabbinical *takana*. But is this not, then, a case in which the sages "uproot" biblical rules? Rabbenu Isaac (known as Ri), one of the most influential Tosafists, puts it this way: "And this is not 'uprooting' anything from the Torah. Since this matter is similar, it is proper to believe. As I explain later on in this chapter [of the talmudic tractate Yevamot], wherever there is some slight reason and support, it is not considered 'uprooting' a regulation of the Torah."[35]

At first sight, all this is shrouded in mystery. Apparently two conditions have to prevail if disregarding a biblical requirement is not to be considered "uprooting": the rabbinical innovation (i.e., *takana*) has to be "similar"; and there must be some "slight reason and support" for it. The "slight reason and support" condition is most surprising. Has it ever been suggested that a rabbinical ruling should "uproot" anything biblical without a reason? On the contrary, there is always some strong reason for it. R. Shimon ben Gamliel's disregard of the husband's right, granted him by the Torah, to annul the *get* even in the absence of his messenger (the example we discussed earlier) is rather compelling. Without it the woman would consider herself divorced while she was still married. (And so it is in all the other examples of this nature discussed in the Talmud. There is always some reason for ignoring the biblical regulation. And yet, they are considered "uprooting.")

Rabbenu Isaac promises that a further explanation of what he has in mind will be found elsewhere in the same chapter. Let us look at it. In discussing the "uprooting" of something found in the Torah, R. Hisda quotes the law regarding the marriage of a minor. It states that if a minor who is married to a *kohen* (a member of the priestly caste) dies, her husband must attend to her funeral, even though he becomes ritually defiled as a result. Now, according to the Torah, a *kohen* must not come in contact with a corpse, either by touching it or even by being with it under the same roof. The exceptions are close relatives who die—among them, of course, his wife. However, a wife who is a minor presents a problem. A minor can be married off only by her father. Nevertheless, the rabbis instituted marriage for a minor orphaned by her father. In order that she be well looked after, the rabbis granted her mother and brothers the right to arrange a marriage for her in her best interest. Such a marriage, however, has no biblical legality. According to biblical law, she is not married, and the man chosen by her family is not her legal husband. How then may a *kohen*, by occupying himself with her burial, "contaminate" himself ritually? This seems to prove R. Hisda's view that the rabbis do have authority to institute regulations contrary to the words of the Torah.

This proof, too, is rejected in the Talmud with the following reasoning: "He is permitted to bury her because she is a *met mitzva*," a corpse whose burial is a commandment of the Torah, obligating even a *kohen*. This needs further elaboration, for a *met mitzva* is defined as a corpse that has nobody to bury it. It is assumed that the wife of the *kohen* has her family to care for her burial. We then hear the final resolution of the problem: "Since it is her husband who inherits her property, she is [as far as her family is concerned] like one who calls but nobody answers her [that being the definition of a *met mitzva*]."[36]

In his comments on this passage, Rabbenu Isaac in the Tosafot argues that the statement that she is a *met mitzva* is not to be taken literally. We know that as there are Israelites around, a *kohen* is not permitted to defile himself by the burial. Even if the family refuses, there are usually other Israelites upon whom the responsibility for her burial devolves. Therefore, maintains Rabbenu Isaac, she is only *like* a *met mitzva*. The rabbis may institute their own rule because it is "a similar case."[37] By combining the two statements of Ri, we are now able to define his principle. A person with whose burial the family will not be concerned is like a *met mitzva*. True, the Torah obligates other Israelites, but in fact she is like "one who calls but is not answered." There is, thus, *reason* to treat her as if she were indeed a *met mitzva*. Such a regulation is, of course, not in agreement with the biblical law, but neither does it "uproot" it. The case being similar to the biblical one, the rabbinical *takana* is an extension of the biblical rule.

In this manner, Tosafot are able to see the rabbinical admission of the various kinds of non-biblical testimonies in the case of the absent husband as not "uprooting" anything biblical. The fact that the woman herself will of necessity carefully investigate the disappearance of her husband makes the presented testimonies similar in their reliability to the testimony of the biblical "two witnesses." What we have here again is the extension of a biblical rule to a similar situation. Why do we do it? Because since there is reason to do it, be it even only a slight reason, it is right and proper to do it. We have here encountered a vital principle of functioning halacha: If there is reason for it, it is "right and proper" to deviate from a biblical regulation in a case that is similar to the one presumed in the Torah; thus, one does not obliterate the regulation, but expands its meaningful applicability.

We have seen how the halacha that the sages have the power to "uproot" biblical requirements only in cases of omission and not in those of commission has been greatly softened. Actually, there is no conclusive proof that that is indeed the unequivocal halachic decision on this subject. Once again we have to refer to a theme we have discussed in a previous section of this study. We have seen that in certain situations the rabbis have the right to annul a marriage retroactively. Usually, the reason for this is expressed in the formula "Everyone who marries does so according to the understanding of the rabbis [i.e., he is aware that the legality of his marriage is determined by the laws and regulations finalized by the halachic authorities]. Thus, [if he violates any of those rules] they invalidate the marriage." On the other hand, we have the story of an incident that happened at a place called Narash. A man forcibly removed a bride from under the wedding canopy before her intended husband, to whom she had been married as a minor, and he then performed a marriage ceremony to make her his wife according to the Torah. The rabbis declared the marriage to the second man, to which the woman ultimately agreed, null and void. By what right could they do that? Since he acted improperly, they, too, acted improperly toward him and annulled his marriage.

In this case as well as in a similar one, the familiar formula that "everyone marries according to the understanding of the rabbis" is missing. As we saw, Rashi and Rashbam in their commentaries were not disturbed by this omission and explained the text as if the usual formula had been tacitly assumed.[38] However, their explanation is not quite convincing, for in both instances, the reason given is that since the man acted improperly, so did the rabbis act improperly toward him by annulling his marriage. This implies that the marriages were valid according to the law but the rabbis acted against the law in annulling them in order to stop such evil practices.

The Tosafot attach importance to the change in the reasoning in both of these apparently exceptional cases. They make the point, for instance, that in the incident at Narash, one cannot really say that the marriage ceremony was performed with the understanding that it be valid in accordance with the rabbinical determination. Right from the beginning, the man who took the bride from her intended husband by force did not consider himself dependent on the approval of the rabbis; he acted against it. But since the woman ultimately agreed to the marriage, it was biblically valid. By annulling it, the rabbis acted against a law of the Torah; they acted "improperly." Comment Tosafot: This shows that, in both these instances, the authorities were of the opinion that the rabbis have the power to "uproot" by commission a biblical law.[39] Shall we perhaps say that in order to uproot evil practices, the rabbis may occasionally limit a biblical commandment?

While the Babylonian Talmud struggles with this issue presented to it by the point of view of R. Hisda, the Jerusalem Talmud asserts unequivocally that the rabbis do have the authority to "uproot" rules of the Torah. [40] Thus, it justifies the view of R. Shimon ben Gamliel that after the *takana* of R. Gamliel the Elder (see above), a husband must not annul a *get*, and if he does, his annulment is ineffective, even though according to biblical law the *get* has become as worthless as a "shard."

The mishnaic source upon which the Jerusalem Talmud bases its justification of R. Shimon ben Gamliel's position is summed up by it as follows:

> Is it not the law of the Torah that one may give *teruma* [the share from the yield of one's land that had to be given to a *kohen*] from olives for what is due for the oil or from grapes for what is due for the wine? Yet they [i.e., the school of Hillel] said one should not do it because of robbing the tribe [of the priests]. What is more, they even went as far as to say that if one violated [their prohibition] the *teruma* is not *teruma* [i.e., it loses its sanctity and may therefore be eaten by a non-*kohen*].

We quote the passage here in its entirety because it is a classic example of what is meant by "uprooting" something that has biblical authority, and because it is almost an exact replica of the original statement of R. Hisda on this theme. According to the law of the Torah, one may calculate the share that is due to the *kohen* from one's olives and oil together or from one's grapes and wine together. One may then give the entire amount from either of them alone, from the olives or from the oil, from the grapes or from the wine. Yet the school of Hillel forbade this practice, because it was "robbing the tribe." If the *kohanim* were given all olives or all grapes, in order to receive their share of oil or wine, the priestly tribe would have to put all the olives in an oil press or all the grapes in a winepress, whereas a portion of its share was pure oil or wine. In other words, while the *kohen* does receive his portion of *teruma*, he suffers a loss because of the work that he would have to invest in order to extract the oil from the olives or the wine from the grapes. The far-reaching significance of the attitude of the school of Hillel lies in the fact that if one trespasses this rabbinical injunction, what was given to the priest loses its character as *teruma*, and (after the *kohen's* share had been separated from the rest of the harvest) it may be eaten by an Israelite. Food of which, according to biblical law, an Israelite was not allowed to partake was thus released to all by rabbinical decree. Here, too, as is the general rule in disagreements between the schools of Shamai and Hillel, the halacha is according to Hillel.

"IT IS TIME TO ACT FOR GOD"

Some aspects of the theme discussed in the previous section show that, in certain other contexts, the talmudic teachers had no doubt that halachic authorities do have the power to suspend the word of the Torah in certain situations. In a long and intellectually exciting discussion with his opponents, R. Hisda quotes the story of the sacrifice that the prophet Elijah offered on Mount Carmel.[41] Elijah was breaking the law, for after the Temple had been built in Jerusalem, one was not permitted to offer sacrifices on any altar outside the holy city. Since Elijah disregarded that law, it shows that the rabbis have the authority to overrule even biblical commandments. One cannot say that only a prophet has that kind of authority, for it is an inviolable principle of the Torah that once the Torah was given no prophet may introduce any innovation. Elijah was therefore not in a category of his own. If he suspended a law, it must be a law that may occasionally be suspended.

This proof of R. Hisda's is also rejected. What Elijah did was done under exceptional circumstances. He built the forbidden altar and sacrificed on it *l'migdar milta*,[42] "to hedge off a situation" that was extremely evil. The people were serving the Baal, the indigenous idol of Canaan. Through the divine service and the miracle that Elijah the prophet performed before the eyes of the people, he prevailed upon them to return to God, to recognize that there is only one God and no one else besides him. Elijah broke the law in order to eliminate a grave evil; that is permissible.

Of course, what we have here is another case of "uprooting." Yet there is an essential difference between this case and those we discussed earlier. To refer once more to the rule of R. Shimon ben Gamliel, the decision to eliminate the husband's right to revoke a *get* even without the knowledge of his messenger to his wife, a right granted to him by the Torah, was meant for all times. That the *shofar* not be blown when Rosh Hashana occurs on the Sabbath became a rabbinical law, binding for all times. Such was also the case in all the other examples that were discussed. Elijah's suspension of the prohibition of altars and sacrifices outside the Temple of Jerusalem was only temporary. "Uprooting" in order to shore up a bad situation, *l'migdar milta*, is allowed only during the duration of an "emergency."

The story of Elijah is not the only one of its kind. Regarding a much later period in Jewish history, R. Elazar ben Yaakov in the Talmud recalls: "I have heard that the rabbinical court may punish not in accordance with [the law of] the Torah, not in order to transgress the Torah but in order to build a fence for the Torah." He continues to tell that "in the days of the Hellenists a man rode a horse on the Sabbath. He was brought before the court and ultimately executed; not because he was worthy of capital punishment, but because the hour demanded it." What R. Elazar says here is that the execution of this man was against the law of the Torah. To ride a horse on the Sabbath is a relatively minor interdict. This man was put to death during "the days of the Hellenists." It happened during a time when the Jewish people were locked in a deadly struggle with the pagan Hellenistic way of life, which claimed many followers and threatened Jewish survival. The man riding a horse on that fateful Sabbath was not just riding a horse; he obviously was a Hellenist flaunting his disregard for the sanctity of the Shabbat. The court was fully aware that it was breaking a biblical law. It did so *l'migdar milta*, to head off a threat to the existence of the Jewish people. This, too, was an act in a temporary, emergency situation, without any validity for the future.

A second form of "uprooting" was also generally admitted. According to the law of the Temple, the priests were not allowed to leave the Temple premises in their priestly garb. The garments were themselves sacred and were to be used only for the service in the Temple, not during any mundane activity. Yet Shimon the Righteous once clad himself in his high priestly clothing and wrapped himself in his high priestly robes and went to receive Alexander the Macedonian (as he is called in the talmudic sources). How was he permitted to do that? The answer is given that he followed a verse in Psalms: "It is time to act for God; they have dissolved your law."[43] The meaning of the answer has to be understood in its midrashic interpretation, which reads the verse like this: "Dissolve the law of God when it is time to act for him." What the high priest Shimon the Righteous did was done for the sake of God. The Gentiles were urging Alexander to destroy the Temple. Shimon went out to meet and pacify him in order to save the Temple. It was a time for Shimon to act for God; therefore, he was allowed to violate the commandment not to leave the Temple in priestly garb.[44]

"It is time to act for God" applies not only in matters directly connected with divine service, like the preservation of the Temple of Jerusalem. At times, it is permitted to suspend a biblical law even by an action whose purpose is altogether social. We read in a mishna: "It was established [by the sages] that one greet one's fellow man with the name of God. For thus we read in the Bible: 'And behold, Boaz came from Bethlehem and said to the harvesters: God be with you.'" This practice, reintroduced in mishnaic times, was not at all self-evident. According to the Torah, one must not take the name of God in vain. To justify this form of greeting, the mishna quotes the verse "It is time to act for God," which one of its teachers, R. Natan, interprets: "Dissolve the law in order to act for God."[45] In this instance, the explanation of Rashi is most revealing. He writes: "At times one abolishes the words of the Torah in order to act for God. So this one, too, whose concern is with the well-being of his fellow man, is doing the will of God. For it is written, 'Seek peace and pursue it.' It is permissible to dissolve the Torah and do what appears to be forbidden."

To some extent this is an exceptional case of "it is time to act for God." There is no real suspension of any law here. Because of a divine commandment, "Seek peace and pursue it," one is actually urged to greet his neighbor with the divine name. Far from taking this name in vain, one actually does the will of God. What one does, then, only appears to violate a commandment. The high priest Shimon acted in a different situation. There was no biblical verse available for him to urge him to go out in his priestly robes when he was attempting to save the Temple from destruction. He had only his own counsel to rely upon, and he had to accept responsibility for temporarily doing away with the law and doing what he had to do for the sake of God. Indeed, Rashi there gives this explanation: "When the time comes to do something for the sake of the Holy One, blessed be he, it is permitted to dissolve the Torah."[46]

This principle is also made use of in an altogether different context. The rule is that the *Torah shebiktav*, the Torah that exists in writing, is not to be turned into oral tradition, and that the *Torah sheb'al peh*, the Oral Torah, must not be committed to writing. Yet we hear that two of the leading rabbis of the Talmud, R. Yohanan and Resh Lakish, were studying part of the oral teaching from a written text. Their behavior is justified on the grounds that one may break the law in order to act for God. Since it became increasingly difficult to commit the entire body of the Oral Torah to memory and thus to preserve it, they said: "Let the Torah be uprooted [i.e., one specific law of it], but let the Torah not be forgotten among Jews." In another passage in the Talmud, the explanation is formulated somewhat differently: "Since it is impossible [i.e., to remember it all], it is time to act for God."

The very same words are also used in another case. At the conclusion of the Torah reading on the Sabbath and festivals, one reads a section from the Prophets, the *haftara*. Some congregations, instead of reading the *haftara* from a complete volume of the prophetical writings, had a special volume containing only the selections that are to be read. That, too, is not to be done; yet they did it. Again the reason is given: "Since it is not possible, it is time to act for God [by trespassing a law]."[47] Rashi explains that to do it otherwise would not have been possible, "because not every congregation could have written the complete set of the Prophets." (This occurred in the period prior to the invention of printing. Complete sets of the handwritten Bible were not readily available. Congregations would write their Bibles themselves, which was often a most difficult undertaking.) Once again we have before us the halachic wisdom of the feasible; only this time the feasible thing is to break a law of the Torah in order to preserve the Torah.

If we now survey the various cases in which the law was suspended for the sake of God, we note that it was due to matters directly connected with the ritual of divine service (the protection of the Temple), for the sake of seeking peace and understanding with one's fellow man (using the name of God when greeting him), and for the sake of doing what is possible in a given situation (protection against physiological shortcomings of human nature [memory], as well as taking into consideration material shortcomings within the communal or social structure [inability to handwrite the complete works of the Prophets]).

It would seem to us that the most original form of "It is time to act for God" is what is called in the Talmud *hora'at sha'a*, a law of the hour. This, too, seems to be in the nature of "uprooting." Yet it is never referred to by this or any similar term.

In the book of Samuel we read that the Philistines, punished for having captured the "Ark of the God of Israel," sent it back on a cart drawn by two cows. The animals found their way to the land of the Jews and brought the cart with the Ark to a place called Beth Shemesh. The people of Beth Shemesh broke up the cart and used the wood to sacrifice the two cows as a burnt offering unto God. The question is discussed: How could they do that? Female animals must not be used for burnt offerings. The problem is resolved by the statement that it was done on the basis of *hora'at sha'a*, a ruling of the hour, only for this occasion.[48] Rashi elaborates that the people were permitted to sacrifice the two cows as a burnt offering "because of the miracle that happened. The cows had found the way by themselves, without being led by a man... they were also singing along the way (based on midrashic interpretation of the biblical text)." The meaning of the "law of the hour" then, is that something unique happened here. When the Torah instructs the Jew that cows are not to be used as burnt offerings, it means that in the normal course of events, it is not to be done. The manner of the return of the Ark from the land of the Philistines turned out to be an extraordinary event, not provided for in the Torah. The people of Beth Shemesh understood that in that hour, in that situation, it was incumbent upon them to acknowledge the miracle by sacrificing the cows to God.

The same solution is offered for similar problems that arose in connection with the return of the Jews from the Babylonian exile under Ezra and Nehemiah. They, too, offered sacrifices.[49] It is said that they did so to atone for the sin of idol worship that the Jews committed in the days of King Zedekiah. Everything about those sacrifices is of a halachically questionable nature. For instance, sacrifices were brought in the Temple for sins committed unintentionally, but they could not be offered for sins committed with full knowledge of what one was doing. But idol worship in the time of Zedekiah was practiced intentionally. The answer is: It was a *hora'at sha'a*, a "law of the hour."

This, however, was not the only deed performed by the Babylonian returnees as a "law of the hour." Agadic tradition says that Ezra, in order to exalt God, pronounced the Tetragrammaton—the *shem hameforash*, the name of God, as it is written in full—at the great national assembly, when he read to the people from the Torah. The law, however, forbids pronouncing God's name in full anywhere outside the precincts of the Jerusalem Temple. This, too, was a "law of the hour."[50] It is obvious that here, too, the occasion was unprecedented. The people returning from Babylon were determined to start a new chapter in the history of the Jewish people. They needed a symbolic expression that they were done with the sins of the past and that this was indeed a new beginning. There was no law for the exceptional historical situation in which they found themselves. They had to create it for that hour. Such was also the occasion at the assembly where they listened to the words of the Torah, read to them by their great teacher Ezra, for the first time after their return to Jerusalem. It was an hour of holy inspiration charged for them all with exceptional meaning and promise. On such an occasion, one does not look into a book of laws, a *Shulhan Aruch*. The laws are meant for the normal, natural course of the life of a people. The moment was more sacred than any Temple service. The unique occasion called for a unique expression. Ezra spoke the holy name of God in its fullness.

Summing up the three categories we have discussed in this section, one would have to say:

1. Wherever there is some evil practice that has to be stopped, an immoral situation that has to be eliminated, one may suspend a specific law and institute measures needed to achieve the necessary improvement. This is the meaning of *l'migdar milta*, "to fence in a thing."

2. When it is necessary to safeguard something of great national or social value, *it is time to act for God*, even by disregarding one law or another.

3. For moments or situations of unique significance in the history of the Jewish people, there can be no prescribed law. To acknowledge their meaning and give them adequate expression, one has to create the "law of the hour," *hora'at sha'a*.

Our discussion brings to mind a saying of Resh Lakish: "At times, the abolition of the Torah is its founding."[51] He bases his idea on a midrashic interpretation. God's reference to the shattering of the Tablets of the Law that Moses received at Sinai suggests, by phonetic association of the Hebrew original, that God actually approved of Moses' bold deed. The daily life and history of the people often confront the teachers of halacha with serious problems for whose solution there are no precedents. Such was the tragic experience of Moses our teacher; while he was still communing with the divine presence on the mountain, in order to receive guidance for the people for all time, the unexpected happened. At a time when their teacher and master had ascended to the ultimate heights of human greatness for their sake, the people below lowered themselves to the degrading worship of the golden calf. How to deal with such a people? How to lead them, in spite of everything, in the ways of Torah and God's commandments? There was no extant answer to such a singular event in human history. The solution had to be found outside the received teaching. In that dark hour, Moses our teacher was all alone. On him alone rested the responsibility of finding the right response to this frightening event. He shattered the tablets he had received from God before the very eyes of the fallen people in order to secure the foundation of the Torah.

CHAPTER THREE

What Is Halacha?

We shall now attempt to sum up the meaning of our analysis. We have examined the ways halacha functions. What does it tell us about the essential nature of halacha?

Halacha is the wisdom of the application of the written word of the Torah to the life and history of the Jewish people. However, this wisdom and its implementation cannot be contained in any book. No written word can deal in advance with the innumerable situations, changes of circumstance, and new developments that normally occur in the history of men and nations. The eternal word of the Torah required a time-related teaching in order to become effective in the life of the Jewish people. This was the tradition passed on by the living word from generation to generation, the *Torah sheb'al peh*, the Oral Torah, beside the *Torah shebiktav*, the Written Torah. The need for it has been clearly described by philosophical as well as halachic authorities. R. Joseph Albo, in his *Ikarim* (*Book of Fundamentals*), explains it as follows:

> The Torah could not be complete in such a manner that it should be adequate for all times. New details are continually

occurring in the affairs of men in customs and actions, too
many to be included in a book. Therefore, God revealed to
Moses orally some general principles, only briefly alluded to
[i.e., in the Written Torah], so that, with their help, the sages
in each generation may deduce the new particulars [of the
law appropriate for the new situation].[1]

While these considerations apply to the entire ambit of
human reality, other commentators emphasized the specifically
ethical aspects of the problem and its solution. Thus, Nahmanides, commenting on the verse "you shall do that which is
right and good in the sight of the Eternal,"[2] has the following to
say:

> ...at first the Torah said, "you shall guard his statutes and
> testimonies which he has commanded you"; now it adds:
> but also in matters about which he did not command you,
> set your mind to doing what is good and right in the eyes of
> God, for he loves the good and the right. This is very impor-
> tant. It is impossible to mention in the Torah the entirety
> of [what should be] human conduct with neighbors and
> friends, in all business activities and all the improvement of
> society and the state. But after a great many of them [i.e.,
> instances of what should be the right conduct in particular]
> are mentioned..., the Torah states generally that one should
> do what is good and right.[3]

Using these remarks of Nahmanides somewhat differently
from the context for which he intended them, one might say
that even the "particulars"—such as "you shall not be a tale-
bearer," "you shall not stand idly by the blood of your neighbor,"

etc.[4]—are generalities that require some understanding of their realization in numerous life situations. Commenting on the biblical words used by Nahmanides, one of the great commentators on the halachic work of Maimonides explains:

> The meaning is that one should conduct oneself properly and with goodness toward one's fellow men. It would not be correct [for the Torah] to command these matters in detail. The Torah was given for all periods and all times and concerning all subjects—and that was necessary. But human qualities and conduct change with the times and the people. So our sages recorded some helpful [decisions regarding] details that they derived from the general principles, some of them as binding laws, others to be done [but without consequences if not done] or recommended as pious deeds.[5]

All three of these authors in a way make clear the need for the Oral Torah to accompany the written word on its journey through the history of the Jewish people. The crystallization of the Oral Torah into a system of teachings and norms for human conduct is the halacha.

By some of the words in our last quotation, one may be guided to an appreciation of another problem present in the application of the Torah to the human condition in its daily reality. In a sense, every system of established law has to cope with a problem that derives from its generality. The law has to formulate general principles, but life situations are always particulars; there is something unique about each of them. In this sense, every law is to some extent "inhuman." The problem is much more serious when the basis of the law is the revealed word of God, which by its very nature is timeless. How can an eternal truth and command take notice of the ever-changing needs of the fleetingly uncertain human condition? God's revelation was not the absolute word of God—which could not be received by any human being—but the word of God addressed to man. However, if that should make any sense, would it not mean the relativization of the absolute?

The problem is further complicated by the fact that the application of the Torah to life throughout the history of the Jewish people had to be entrusted to man. It had to be, because "the Torah was given not to God's ministering angels" but to mere man. Once the Torah was revealed to the children of Israel, its realization on earth became their responsibility, to be shouldered by human ability and human insight. That is, we suggest, the ultimate meaning of R. Yehoshua's bold stand: "The Torah is no longer in heaven!"[6] One pays no attention to a voice from heaven in matters of the realization of Torah on earth. So is it intended and explicitly stated in the Torah itself. It could not be otherwise. The divine truth had to be poured into human vessels; it had to be "humanized." Having left its heavenly abode, it had to be accommodated in the modest cottages of human uncertainty and inadequacy. This, in essence, is the task of the halacha. The "humanization" of the word of God requires that in applying the Torah to the human condition, one takes into consideration human nature and its needs, human character and its problems, the human condition in its ever-fluctuating dimension, the Jew and the Jewish people in their unique historical reality.

We have gained some insight into how this task is accomplished by halacha. As the "wisdom of the feasible," halacha safeguards the effective, pragmatic functioning of the economic and social structure of an autonomous Jewish society. We have also seen how, in a conflict between the consequences of a law in a specific case and the ethical demand in that case, the ethical element is given sufficient authority to modify or curb the applicability of the law. We observed it especially in the halachic effort to strengthen the rather inadequate status of the woman as it appears in the written Torah. It was done to the extent that in certain cases a way was found to *compel* a husband to divorce his wife of *his free will*, thus, on one hand, ensuring that the wife is freed from an intolerable bond, and on the other, not violating the biblical law that a *get* (writ of divorce) has to be given freely by the husband. In other cases, to protect a woman from becoming an *aguna* (i.e., married to a non-existent husband), reason was found not to apply the biblical law of testimonies that requires two witnesses. One of the most far-reaching efforts in this area was the basis of the halachic authority to annul a marriage retroactively.[7]

No less significant is the effort to render the application of the Torah to life relevant to the contemporary situation. To recall just one example: In the Torah the *halitza* ceremony was instituted only as a way out for a recalcitrant brother-in-law who refused to marry the widow of his brother who died without leaving any children. However, when mores changed, the halacha gave preference to *halitza* over *yibum* (levirate marriage), some authorities discouraging the latter, others even forbidding it. The requirement of contemporaneous relevance found expression in the midrashic reading of a verse in Psalms that yielded: "It is time to act for God; let them dissolve the Torah."[8] It has also been formulated in the two other guiding

principles we have discussed. As to the personal responsibility of
the halachic authority, one teaches: "A *dayan* should decide in
accordance with his own understanding of the case before him";
concerning the public's attitude toward the halachic authority,
the other states: "You have only the judge of your own days to
turn to."[9]

This latter view we shall quote in full as it has been formulated in the Talmud.[10] In one place in the Bible, the early judges
in Jewish history—Jerubbaal, Bedan, and Jephthah—are cate-
gorized with the prophet Samuel;[11] in another passage, Samuel
is compared to Moses and Aaron.[12] The logical rule of identity
that if A = B and B = C, then A = C gives us the midrashic equa-
tion that:

> The Torah has equated three scarcely significant personali-
> ties [i.e., the three judges] with three highly important ones
> [i.e., Moses, Aaron, and Samuel] to tell you that Jerubbaal
> in his generation is like Moses in his; Bedan in his time like
> Aaron in his; Jephthah in his days like Samuel in his own.
> This is to teach you that once a person has been appointed
> "the provider" for the community, may he be ever so insignif-
> icant, he is like the mightiest among the mighty. And so it is
> also said: "And you shall come unto the priests, the Levites,
> and unto the judges that shall be in those days."[13]

How could it have occurred to anyone to go to a judge not living in his own days? (In other words, what need was there to
emphasize "the judge that shall be in those days"?) This means
to say: You have to go only to (i.e., to inquire only of) the judge
of your own time. Furthermore, it is said: "Do not say: 'How

was it that the former years were better than these?'" Thus says the Talmud. Ecclesiastes continues: "for it is not out of wisdom that you inquire concerning this."[14] The word of God has to be rendered meaningful in each generation. That is the secret of its eternal validity.

It is obvious that halacha in its essential nature is the most potent antidote to fundamentalism. But is not the human share in it too overwhelming? We have seen how some biblical commandments, such as those concerning the "rebellious son" and the "idolatrous city," were completely abrogated.[15] A superficial study may give the impression that often, instead of rejecting a biblical command outright, the halacha attempts to get around it. For instance, instead of saying that we cannot accept the cancellation of all debts every seventh year because it is unworkable, Hillel introduced his *takana* of the *prozbul*.[16]

Let us consider the method by which halachic innovations are introduced or the law of the Torah is applied to a concrete situation. We shall use a halachic example known as "the share of sons in the *ketuba* of their mother," or, in talmudic language, *ketubat b'nin dichrin*. This was a *takana*, a regulation introduced by the sages, that a husband should undertake that in case his wife died before him and he inherited her, he in turn would bequeath his wife's inherited dowry to the sons he had by her, as their inheritance. This made sense in a polygamous society. By such an undertaking only the mother's children would ultimately inherit the dowry she brought into the marriage. Without it, all the children of the father would share in the estate.

Why was the *takana* introduced? The Talmud explains: "So that a father would be ready to give to his daughters as would ultimately be received by his sons [i.e., after his death]." That is, if a father knows the dowry he gives his daughters will ultimately be inherited exclusively by her children, his grandchildren, he will be willing to commit himself in his daughter's *ketuba* to a far larger dowry than he would otherwise.

However, such an arrangement changes, in a sense, the biblical law of inheritance, since for the sake of a richer dowry for his daughter, the father withdraws a portion of his possessions that ultimately would become part of the estate to be inherited by his sons. The Talmud continues the discussion: "How can such a thing be possible? The Torah says the sons inherit, not the daughters, but the rabbis introduced a regulation that daughters inherit too?" This seems to be a *takana* directed against the biblical law. To which we hear the surprising answer: "This too is a biblical law. It is written—Jeremiah advised the exiles in Babylon—'take yourselves wives and beget sons and daughters; take wives for your sons, and give your daughters to husbands.'"[17] The meaning of this advice is interpreted thus:

> "Take wives for your sons" we understand, for it is customary for the man to go and look for a wife; but "give your daughters to husbands," how is that to be understood? It is not customary for daughters to offer themselves in marriage. How, then, is this part of the prophet's advice to be followed? What Jeremiah suggests is: clothe her [one's daughter] and provide for her, so men will be eager to come and marry her.[18]

We have before us a principle of halachic legislation. There is indeed a biblical law that sons inherit their father's estate (the daughters were to be provided for differently). However, that is not the only concern of the Torah. The care for the well-being of the daughters is no less a biblical command. It appears clearly in Jeremiah's message to the exiles. It does not contradict the law of inheritance; it limits its applicability. This, too, is a biblical command.

Earlier we discussed the *takana* of using the divine name when greeting a fellow man.[19] It was based on the principle of disregarding the Torah when it is time to act for God. Let us once again consider Rashi's interpretation:

> At times one abrogates words of the Torah in order to act for God. So in this case, too. To inquire about the well-being of another person [by greeting him with God's name] one is doing the will of God, for it is written: "Seek peace and pursue it." It is permitted to dissolve Torah and do what appears to be forbidden.

The key words in this explanation are "what appears to be forbidden." The law says that one must not take the name of God in vain, but there is also another divine command: "Seek peace and pursue it." In the understanding of the sages, the more comprehensive law enlightens us as to the meaning of taking God's name in vain.

One might say that this is an essential aspect of halachic methodology. It informs, for instance, the entire subject of "uprooting" a law of the Torah. We discussed at length and in a different context the decision of R. Shimon ben Gamliel that if a husband sends his wife a *get* by messenger but trespasses upon the *takana* of R. Gamliel the Elder and invalidates the *get* before it reaches her, informing neither the messenger nor the wife, his act takes no effect and his wife is duly divorced. This abrogates the biblical law in this matter.

We saw that according to the Jerusalem Talmud as well as in the view of R. Hisda in the Babylonian one, this indicates that the rabbis have the authority to "uproot" a law of the Torah.[20] However, if we look carefully, the legal philosophy behind the principle may reveal that the word "uprooting" is not to be taken too literally.

Within the system of biblical divorce, a husband may annul a divorce document he has sent his wife before it reaches her. Once again, this is not the entire Torah. There are situations in which the application of this law may lead to dire consequences for a wife. For instance, if the husband invalidates the *get* without his wife's knowledge, and she then receives it from a messenger, she has every reason to assume she is divorced; yet she is not. Should she then, in good faith, enter into another marriage, she commits adultery. The Torah dare not ignore such a possibility. Apart from the rights of the husband, the vital interests of the wife have to be taken into consideration. To protect her is also the will of God, as revealed in the Torah. One is not really "uprooting" a law of the Torah; one is limiting its application using the authority of the Torah itself. The more comprehensive biblical command—in this case, "you shall love your neighbor as yourself"—teaches how and when to apply the specific law regarding the husband's right to invalidate a *get*.

We might say that the entire subject matter of halacha as "The Priority of the Ethical" in chapter 1 is based on the comprehensive description of the nature of the Torah as found in the Torah itself: "Its ways are ways of pleasantness, and all its paths are peace."[21] We may add that, in a similar sense, the halachic determinations regarding the practicality and effective functioning of the material, economic, and social structure of Jewish existence are the realization of the biblical injunction "And you shall live by them," by the commandments of God. In pursuit of the meaning of this and similar Torah injunctions, halacha became the wisdom of the feasible.[22]

The interpretation we are offering here has already, in essence, been formulated by the sixteenth- and seventeenth-century scholar R. Shlomo Eliezer Eideles (known as Maharsha) in his novellae (*hidushim*) at the end of the talmudic tractate Yevamot. That volume ends with a saying by R. Eliezer in the name of R. Hanina: "The disciples of the wise (*talmidei hachamim*) increase peace in the world, as it is written, 'all your children shall be taught by the Eternal; and great shall be your children's peace.'"[23]

This concluding remark of the tractate seems to have no connection with what immediately precedes it in the text. Maharsha explains the reason for this strange conclusion as follows:

> This tractate contains a number of rather surprising statements that seem to "uproot" something from the Torah. In one chapter, the question is raised in several cases whether a rabbinical court has the authority to uproot anything from the Torah. An answer is given. At the beginning of that chapter, regarding the leniency practiced in order to save a woman from becoming an *aguna*, Tosafot explain that it is not a matter of "uprooting," for the case is similar, and it is also right and proper to do it.[24] But that is unconvincing. So, too, concerning our present subject [discussed at the close of the tractate Yevamot], how could they have been so lenient as to abolish a rule of the Torah? For the law is that witnesses have to be subjected to rigorous, probing

examination [in other words, according to what is taught there, the "rigorous, probing examination" is dispensed with where the testimony pertains to an absent husband].

A number of similar examples are further listed.[25] To answer these questions, says Maharsha, this tractate concludes with the saying that "The disciples of the wise increase peace in the world,"

> as if to say that all these rabbinic regulations do not uproot anything from the Torah. All this is concerned with the virtue of peace.... This is not uprooting but realizing the virtue of peace in that a woman does not become an *aguna* or [in other cases, where a woman is freed from the *halitza* ceremony] a wife may not appear displeasing in the eyes of her husband [because of the stigma of *halitza*], lest he divorce her.

Such would not be the ways of pleasantness or the paths of peace.

We have seen it to be a well-established form of functioning halacha that when a specific law conflicts with another, supervening concern of the Torah, one does the will of God by eliminating the specific law in the case at hand. However, interpreting and deciding in all these matters has been entrusted to the sages of Israel. Their contribution to the interpretation and application of the Torah through the ages is itself part of the Torah. To refer once again to the great discussion between R. Eliezer and his colleagues, when R. Yehoshua rose up and declared, "The Torah is no longer in heaven; we pay no attention to a heavenly voice," he was able to make that stand supported by biblical authority. He gave his reason: It is a command of the Torah, in all cases of differing opinions, to decide according to the majority. In this manner the Torah itself recognizes the authenticity of differing interpretations as well as the resolution of such disagreement by human authority. It is the divine recognition of the human share in the living Torah (*Torat hayim*), in the Torah in its phase of realization in the life of the Jewish people, as it was originally intended in the act of its revelation.

The human share in the Torah is also manifest in the importance attached to *sevara*, man's reasoning ability. We found that any principle or idea whose soundness can be established by reason is sufficiently authoritative so as not to require biblical validation. Two of the only three commandments for which a Jew is to sacrifice his life rather than transgress are derived from a law to which the biblical text itself refers as known and acknowledged on the strength of a *sevara*.[26]

It is, however, important to understand that the human reason whose insights and deductions the halacha recognizes is not what is known as reason in the Western tradition, especially in philosophical idealism. It is not absolute or universal reason. There is no need for us to enter into a discussion here as to whether that kind of reason is at all accessible to human beings. We have given sufficient indication in this study that this author knows only human reason. The *sevara* that has such an important function in halacha is that kind of reason; it is neither absolute nor universal. This, too, we have learned from R. Yehoshua's stand in that fateful discussion. Was the voice from heaven mistaken when it announced to the sages that in all matters of disagreement between them the halacha is like R. Eliezer's opinion? Did it not know the truth? That great assembly of the teachers of Israel could not have thought so. Of course, the voice was right. Its pronouncement was true; it was absolute truth. That is why it could not be accepted on earth. The affairs of a people on earth cannot be guided by a permanent hot line to the heavens.

As we have seen, differences of interpretation and modes of realization of the Torah have been envisaged by the Torah itself since its inception. Majority rule is of necessity the will of the Torah. But truth determined by majority vote is not objective truth; it is only pragmatic truth. Thus, we have found that when the opinion even of an individual teacher is based on a *sevara* that appears sound, it is accepted as halacha against a majority. Similarly, when a minority is overruled, its view is not suppressed but, rather, kept on record for a time when it may become logically convincing. Even regarding the "rebellious elder," who refuses to acknowledge the ruling of the Sanhedrin, while he is not permitted to break the law or teach others to break it, he is allowed to continue teaching his own point of view. Conceivably, one day even this opinion might become the accepted halacha. Intellectual tolerance goes hand in hand with the realization that the Torah is no longer in heaven.

While the interpretation and application of the Torah to life could not dispense with the instrument of human reason, it would seem that the human share in its totality controlled the ways in which reason was to be used. In our study thus far, we have been able to observe a number of inconsistencies. One was in the handling of the principle of "Where it is possible (*heicha de'efshar*), it is possible; where it is not possible, it is not possible."

We shall cite one example we examined earlier.[27] When a man hands his wife a *get* that is to take effect immediately before his death (thereby freeing her from the bonds of levirate marriage), his wife—if he is a *kohen* and she eats *teruma* as his wife—is forbidden to partake of *teruma* as soon as the *get* is handed to her. Her husband may die any minute, so the present may be the moment immediately preceding his death. Whereas when a husband, old or sick, sends a *get* to his wife through a messenger, it may be handed to her to be divorced. Since her husband was alive when he sent it, we assume he is alive now as well, so he may divorce his wife.

In one case, we reckon with the ever-present mortality of man; in the other, we disregard it. According to one explanation, the reason is simple. In the case of the wife whose husband is a *kohen*, she need only refrain from partaking of *teruma*, permitted only to a *kohen* and his family. But there are other kinds of food available to her. That is then feasible. However, in the case of an old or sick man in a distant country or city, sensing the approach of his end, if he knew that the *get* he wished to send would have no validity, he would, of course, not go to the trouble of sending one at all. Thus, his wife might become an *aguna*. This is something not to be contemplated.

We have here what might be called a case of logical inconsistency. In one case, halacha takes into consideration the human condition of mortality; in the other, it disregards it completely. Even more striking is the absence of attention given to the logical requirement of consistency in the halachic interpretation of some biblical texts. Again we quote from material already discussed. According to biblical law, a man is not permitted to remarry his former wife if after their divorce she married another man, who then divorced her. We saw that the rabbis applied the law even if her second marriage was never consummated (halachically speaking, there was only *erusin*—a halachically binding engagement—but no *nisuin*). This seems to contradict the plain meaning of the biblical text that says, "since she had been defiled." Surely this means that she actually lived with her second husband, but not when they were married only by *erusin*, the halachically binding engagement. The rabbis are not disturbed by the plain meaning of the text. The words "she had been defiled" refer only to the case of a *sota*, a woman suspected of adultery. So they explain it. This "interpretation" flies completely in the face of the entire context in which the words occur. Nothing is mentioned there about a *sota*. We noted that Tosafot explained that the rabbis could not accept the plain meaning of the text because they could not make peace with the idea that a divorced woman who marries another man becomes defiled by that marriage. They therefore imposed their "interpretation" on the text.[28]

In other cases, there is insistence on the plain meaning of the text. Once again we shall refer to the case of the "rebellious son," who was brought to the rabbinical court by his parents and whose punishment was to have been death.[29] This law was interpreted out of existence by the strictest adherence to the literal idiosyncrasy of the text. The parents, as they deliver their son into the hands of the court, have to declare, among other things, "he does not listen to our voice." The word "voice" is understood in its physical meaning. Since the Bible does not say "our voices," but "our voice," father and mother must have the same voice, both speaking at the same pitch, sounding alike. And if they must have the same voice, they must be alike; alike in size and appearance. It is most unlikely that such physical similarity between parents ever occurs. The conclusion, therefore, is: "The case of the rebellious son never was; never will one ever be. It was written to be [correctly] interpreted and be rewarded [i.e., for its elimination by interpretation]."

In one example, utter disregard for the plain meaning of the text; in the other, adherence to the literal wording ad absurdum. There is not always logical consistency in the use of *sevara*. The *sevara* is not theoretical reasoning. It is the human intellect functioning within the embracing socio-ethical context of the halacha. It is practical reason in the sense that it requires consistency in the halachic endeavor to realize halacha's two guiding ideals, as presented to it by the Torah: "You shall live by them [by God's commandments] and not die by them," and "Its ways are ways of pleasantness, and all its paths are peace."

There is in the human share in the Torah, without which halacha would be impossible, a great measure of independence granted to the teachers of the Torah, as well as a strong portion of relativism introduced into the interpretation of the word of God revealed at Sinai. However, both are integrated into the very essence of the Torah. That is the ultimate meaning of the statement, also revealed by a heavenly voice, that "these as well as those are the words of the living God."[30] It is a matter of coordination between the revealed word of God and the human world. The coordination is possible because the word of man in this case is a "disciple" of the revealed one. The teachers of Israel are committed to the Torah from Sinai. They heard the voice and absorbed the tradition of Israel's effort through the ages to render the bequest of the tablets life-guarding and life-forming. When they then speak their word in accordance with their understanding, they indeed teach one of the "forty-nine facets" of the Torah given to man at Sinai.

One of the most impressive examples of this coordination between the divine commandment and its human understanding and realization in a concrete life situation is the creative insight of the Tosafist Rabbenu Isaac, who deemed it proper to apply to a problem new solutions, not provided for in the Torah, if the novelty serves a purpose similar to the one aimed at by the biblical law. Thus, in the case of the wife who was a minor, her husband, a *kohen*, was made responsible for her burial as if she had been his wife according to biblical rules (which, as a minor without a father, she could not be). She was treated as a *met mitzva*, a person who died without leaving any relatives, and no other Israelite was available to bury her. Even though technically she was not a *met mitzva*, for there were relatives and other Israelites who were obligated to occupy themselves with her burial, in fact—since her husband inherits her fortune—no one would accept responsibility for her burial. She was therefore like a *met mitzva*. The purpose at which the Torah aimed was served in this case, though not in accordance with the literal meaning of the biblical law.

In the same way, one is to understand the dispensing by the rabbis with the biblical requirement of two witnesses in order to save a woman from becoming an *aguna*. True, the law says that a fact is to be established on the basis of the testimony of two witnesses, yet the essential point is that the fact be ascertained. In this case there is justification for considering the fact established even by a form of testimony not otherwise admitted. Since there is a human need to do so, we act accordingly.[31] In essence, what is being done is a broadening of the possibility of serving a biblical purpose by new laws not provided for in the Torah.

The Talmud expresses the idea of the integration of the human element in the Torah with the revealed word by a saying of R. Yohanan. Basing himself on the literal meaning of the Hebrew, he reads a verse in Exodus in the following manner: "...for in accordance with these spoken words have I concluded a covenant with you and Israel."[32] Words of a covenant are not dictates from on high. They are spoken in the intimacy of mutual affirmation and acceptance. They invite man to make his own contribution and to accept his share of responsibility. Halacha is the final outcome of this covenantal mutuality of recognition.

The significance of all this for the Jew of today may be illustrated by the contemporary problem of values and ethics. In one of his dicta on ethics, Immanuel Kant makes the statement that "it does not seem surprising that all previous attempts to find the principle of morality should have ended in failure." Kant was of the opinion that man knows he is duty-bound to obey a "universal system of law" but does not understand the source of that law. His solution was that "good will" is the authority, that "the universal system of laws to which he [i.e., man] is subject are laws which he imposes upon himself," and that "he is only under obligation to act in conformity with his own will, a will which by the purpose of nature prescribes universal laws." On that basis, Kant is able to write: "The supreme principle of morality I shall, therefore, call the principle of the autonomy of the will, to distinguish it from all other principles, which I call principles of heteronomy."[33] Needless to say, a law commanded by God, usually referred to as theonomous, is one form of heteronomy. In our own day Sartre, too, spoke of "the autonomy of the will" when he maintained that man is the creator of his own values. With this, Sartre, like Kant, was also rejecting any kind of heteronomy. But whereas Kant believed that man's will was the supreme principle of a universal system of laws, Sartre denied the very idea of a universal law.

Kant's theory would be acceptable if the will of man were indeed the supreme principle of a "universal system of laws." The fact is that there is no such thing as *the* will of man. There are innumerable human wills, in their majority differing from each other and none of them separable from its essential subjectivity. Because of that, they cannot serve as "the supreme principle of morality," as Kant understood the term. Whatever Sartre thought of a "supreme principle of morality," the ultimate logic of his position is very similar to the one inherent in Kant's. *Man* as a creator of his values just does not exist. There is no man in the abstract; there are only men. And if they are all creators of their values, then this "supreme principle of morality" is responsible for innumerable values or systems of laws, often not only differing from each other but actually contradicting one another, and each claiming the authority of the autonomous will.[34] Autonomy thus degenerates into everyone's "doing his own thing." The result is social and international decadence.

If, then, for the purposes of our own theme, we concentrate on heteronomy in the sense of a revealed system of law, the confrontation between autonomy and theonomy appears in a new sense. It is the collision between a relativism that leads to social as well as international decadence and a barren fundamentalism that stifles human nature. In the mutuality of the covenant, theonomy and autonomy serve together a common purpose. The supreme principle of the law to which man is subject is theonomous, its ultimate source of authority being will of God; the interpretation of the law and its application to innumerable and forever-changing life situations are autonomous. Theonomy liberates the human will from the potentially destructive relativism of its subjectivity; human autonomy protects the absoluteness of the law against the occasionally negative consequences of its time-alienated objectivity. Through halacha the word from Sinai has become the way of life of the Jewish people throughout history.

CHAPTER FOUR

Halacha in Our Time

HALACHA IN EXILE

With the destruction of the Second Temple and the collapse of the Jewish commonwealth, both the Jewish people and its entire spiritual world went into exile. The Oral Torah and the halacha lost their natural habitat. Judaism was meant to be the total way of life of the Jewish people. It comprehends the entire manifestation of a national existence, its political and economic structure, its socio-ethical goals, its spiritual vision, and its cultural strivings. Judaism is not a religion but a comprehensive religious civilization; it is not a church but the process of realization through world history of the potential essence of a unique people. For its fulfillment it requires a national framework within which the Jewish people is independent and in control of its own life. With the exile, that framework was shattered.

Since halacha is the wisdom of application of the words of the Torah, its teachings and commandments, to the real-life situation of the Jewish people, the field of application narrows to the extent to which control over their lives falls from the hands of the people. For instance, because of the exile of the Jewish people in the years 69–70 of the common era, all the halachot connected with the possession of the land (e.g., *teruma*, *ma'aser*, *pe'a*, the sabbatical year) froze at a level appropriate to the agricultural and economic order of that period. It is impossible to know what form of realization they would have received had those areas of national existence been allowed to develop normally in a Jewish state, extending into our own days of mechanized agriculture as part of an internationally linked and interdependent economic order.

The classical purpose of halacha is to shape the Jewish realities of the life of a people. In exile, halacha is confronted with the problems, needs, and demands of non-Jewish realities forced upon a people scattered into communities in the midst of cultures and civilizations alien to the spirit and ideals of Judaism. The demands of the Jewish realities upon halacha are Jewish even in their problematic nature; those of the non-Jewish realities are anti-Jewish. For instance, the Sabbath does not stand by itself. It is the conclusion of a temporal rhythm that is preceded by six working days beginning on Sunday. In the midst of a civilization whose official day of rest is Sunday, the Sabbath does not link up naturally with the rest of the week. In fact, it often becomes a disturbing element.

In exile, the encounter between Torah and reality is a confrontation; in an autonomous Jewish civilization, it is a challenge. In the situation of confrontation, the task of halacha is preservation: how to preserve the life of the people and its Jewish character in the midst of a politically mostly inimical and spiritually and morally alien world. Halacha in exile is essentially protective halacha, often on the defensive. In meeting the challenge of a comprehensive Jewish civilization, halacha develops its creative originality. Hence the statement that there is no Torah like the Torah of the land of Israel.[1] The Torah needs the call from the autonomous reality of the Jewish people. In halachic response to the needs and problems of that reality, it is enabled to speak the timely word of its eternal wisdom in each changing situation.

It should, however, be noted that the intensity of the exile of the halacha does not exactly coincide with the loss of political sovereignty in the Jewish land. As long as a rich measure of civic autonomy existed, and Jews settled the land en masse, halacha could still flourish. This was the case for several generations even after the destruction of the Temple. The situation was similar for several centuries in Babylon till the conclusion of the Talmud. There internal Jewish autonomy was given governmental authority. Large areas of the country were settled by Jews, who engaged in all the occupations, trades, and professions that are normal in any society. However, as the internal autonomy was gradually reduced in the Jewish communities in the diaspora, as they were forced from the land and limited in their occupational activities, the potential application of the Torah to a life that was Jewish in its material and spiritual structure became limited. As we approach modern times, important sections of the halacha cease to function. Almost everything that deals with the judiciary, with criminal and civic law, becomes a mere intellectual exercise without any involvement in actual life situations. As forms of internal Jewish autonomy wither, the public domain of halachic implementation of the Torah in the life of the people shrinks. More and more, halacha is forced into the private domain of the family, the synagogue, the congregation, the Jewish school.

These, then, are the characteristics of halacha in exile: because of the confrontation with an essentially non-Jewish reality, halacha is forced on the defensive; unchallenged by an autonomous Jewish reality, halacha is compelled to remain silent on issues that are vital within the structure of a national civilization. Notwithstanding, halacha functioned successfully in exile, serving the needs of the Jewish people there. But just as exile is an unnatural political and material condition for the people, it is an unnatural spiritual condition for halacha. Of necessity, exile saps halacha's creative originality.

We have discussed thus far what we may call the exile of halacha from reality. However, another form of exile has been forced upon halacha. Torah was handed down from generation to generation by the living word of human understanding as Oral Torah. It crystallized into halacha. Thus, the Torah from heaven became Torah for the earth.

As we have seen, human understanding of and capacity for meaningful implementation were called into contributing participation in the Torah through the mutuality of the covenant concluded with Israel by means of the Oral Torah. Halacha is the result of the cooperation between the eternal written word and the timely spoken one. A text solidifies a meaning; the spoken word of wisdom carries within itself the awareness of its situation-dependent validity as well as the vitality of self-renewal. Therein lies the significance of the law that forbade entrusting the Oral Torah to writing.[2] The eternal word of the Torah may speak with timely meaningfulness to all generations of the Jewish people because of the ever-present capacity for self-renewal of the Oral Torah.

Such is the ideal situation. Unfortunately, as a result of the destruction of the Second Jewish Commonwealth and the dispersion of the Jewish people from its homeland, the situation changed radically. Because of external necessity, the Oral Torah solidified. It became increasingly difficult to entrust the entire, accumulated oral teaching to memory. The problem was aggravated beyond all proportion by political upheavals and uncertainties. As a first step, the Oral Torah had to be systematized. This process reached its brilliant conclusion in the Six Orders of the Mishna, edited by R. Yehuda Hanasi. In it, Rabbenu Hakadosh—as he was also called—assembled from a much richer tradition all the teachings that he and his court considered to be most authentic. Later authorities disagree as to whether the Six Orders were actually committed to writing by R. Yehuda himself or much later, upon the redaction of the Talmud. Be that as it may, the transformation of the halachic tradition into a systematic and authoritative work was in itself a revolutionary departure from the norm.

R. Yehuda Hanasi undertook this task, says Maimonides, lest the "Oral Torah be forgotten in Israel." This formulation draws on what the Talmud explains about how R. Yohanan and Resh Lakish were able to study agada from a book, though the law forbids putting the oral teaching into writing. As we saw, it was a "time to act for God": let the law be dissolved, but let not the Torah be forgotten in Israel.[3] However, Maimonides understood that the danger of forgetting lay mainly not in the natural frailties of man's memory but in the unpropitious conditions of the time:

Why did Rabbenu Hakadosh act that way and not leave things as they were? He saw that the number of disciples continued to diminish, and ever-new troubles were afoot. The power of Rome was spreading and gaining strength in the world, and the Jewish people were wandering to the ends of the earth. He therefore composed one volume to be placed into the hands of them all, that they may learn it fast and that it not be forgotten.[4]

The Talmud, essentially an interpretation of the Mishna, was finalized and written down in 500 c.e., about three hundred years after the work of R. Yehuda Hanasi, The reasons for the formal conclusion of the Talmud were similar to those that inspired R. Yehuda's compilation. The time of the flourishing of the great talmudic academies was over. The most important among them, Sura and Pumpedita, had been closed by the authorities. It was a period of persecution and anarchy in Babylon. Even though the two most important schools reopened temporarily, the Jewish communities were deteriorating. The systematization of the new material collected in the Talmud, started by Rav, was completed under Ravina. The main body of the Oral Torah, which was never meant to become a text, had thus been transformed into another kind of written Torah. This result was not due to developments from within the oral tradition, but—contrary to its essential nature—was forced upon it by the power of extrinsic, inimical circumstances.

We call this development the exile of the Oral Torah into literature. After the redaction of the Talmud, the process of interpretation continued. The written word can be rendered meaningful only by interpretation. More and more insights and concepts accumulated. But now, in the post-talmudic period, an entirely new phase in the history of the Oral Torah commenced:

that of its codification. While various principles govern how to reach halachic decisions,[5] the Mishna itself is not a code. It contains discussions and quotes numerous opinions in disagreement with each other. This is even truer of the Gemara, which constitutes by far the greatest part of the Talmud.

The very idea of codification violates the essence of the Oral Torah. According to one formulation in the Talmud, those who write down halachot are like people who burn the Torah.[6] "These as well as those are the words of the living God" would be an intellectual and moral monstrosity within a code of law. But again, conditions detrimental to the preservation of the tradition seem to have been the determining factor in this new phase. The process of codification reached its most authoritative forms in the code of Maimonides, the *Tur* by R. Jacob ben Asher, and the *Shulhan Aruch* by R. Joseph Karo.

The reasons that induced Maimonides to transform the entire body of halacha into a code were again similar to those that prevailed at the time of the conclusion of the Mishna and Talmud. He refers to the severe troubles and pressures of the times, which decreased understanding of the halachic works of the post-talmudic gaonic period. Nor were most people able to apply themselves to the study of the Talmud with the intensity needed to grasp the ramifications for halachic conduct. Therefore, Maimonides composed his code

in clear and easily understandable language... so that all the laws be open to [the understanding] of small and great alike in the matter of all the commandments and all the regulations of the sages and prophets... so that no person be in need of consulting any other work regarding all the laws of Israel; but this work be the compendium of the entire Oral

Torah, including the [rabbinical] regulations, customs, and edicts that were developed since the days of Moses up to the compilation of the Gemara and as they were interpreted by the Geonim in all their works that they authored since the conclusion of the Talmud.

The author of the *Tur*, in the introduction to his *Hoshen Hamishpat* on Jewish jurisprudence, points to another feature of exile that led him to undertake the task of codification. He reminds the reader that in former times there were lower and higher courts all over Israel that in all cases of disagreement in interpretation or theory ruled with constitutional authority. During our long exile all that had disappeared, and one was bogged down in a multitude of contradictory and confusing opinions. He therefore found it necessary to write his classifying code.

The code of Maimonides has remained to this day the most original and impressive masterpiece in all halachic literature, the unique creation of a unique genius. Most probably it has been the most influential work in saving the entire body of the Oral Torah from disintegration amidst the destructive pressures of exile. It has been the lifeline of Jewish survival. Yet there could hardly be anything further removed from the original nature and purpose of the Oral Torah than a work that dispenses with all older sources of the Oral Torah. It is unavoidable exile halacha, forced upon the Oral Torah by external conditions beyond its control. The codification of the halacha is another case of "dissolve the Torah in order to act for God." No wonder that the very idea of codification excited a great deal of opposition.[7] Codification is contrary to the very nature of halacha. It works like shackles upon its halacha's creative vigor. Such was the price of Jewish survival and the preservation of Jewish identity in exile.

The history of the Oral Torah contains several milestones. Once the Mishna was concluded, it was determined that subsequent sages could only interpret the Mishna but not disagree with it. In cases of disagreement, one would have to find support in the opinion of a teacher of the Mishna. Since the redaction of the Talmud, no one is permitted to disagree with its teachings. Undoubtedly, these were protective measures dictated by exilic conditions. Had Jewish national existence been able to continue normally in the land of Israel, it is doubtful whether there would have been a formal conclusion of the mishnaic period. One may ponder what form of talmudic-type Mishna interpretation would have developed, without ever reaching even the semblance of an answer. These authority barriers seem to depart from the rule of the Torah, with which we have already become familiar, that one must turn to the "judge" of his own days.[8] Indeed! Except that the "judge of our own days" does not exist. He could function only within the constitutional judiciary system of the Jewish people living in its own land.[9]

The exilic form in which the Oral Torah and with it halacha have reached us may indicate the seriousness of the problem confronting a Jewry that believes its future lies in halachic Judaism. The twofold exile of halacha—from reality and into literature and codification—forced it into a straitjacket as we face the challenges of our time. Nowhere is this felt more severely than in the modern State of Israel. After almost two millennia of exile, halacha has been given back its authentic partner, the daily reality of the life of a Jewish people living in its own land. It is the commanding opportunity for the realization of the Torah of the land of Israel, which is like no other Torah.

Halacha has once again a comprehensive form of Jewish reality to work with, a broad field of Torah application to life—political, economic, social, ethical. Once again, Torah may move from the private, congregational domain to which exile had limited it into the public domain of a nation. Halacha, which in exile had to be on the defensive, building fences around communal islands, now ought to resume its classical function and originate new forms of relevant Torah realization in the State of Israel. It should concern itself with questions of social justice, economic honesty, and fairness, with problems of labor relations and the work ethos, with the social gap, with ethics and morality in public life, even with such matters as traffic laws in the cities and on the highways. How is the Sabbath to be observed in a highly industrialized society that depends on continuous-process industries that cannot be turned off every Friday at sunset? Are they to be serviced only by non-religious Jews, just as the police force, for instance, is to be recruited only from among non-Sabbath-observant citizens? Is this what the Torah intended by a Jewish people living in its own land, a land dependent on the Jewish "*shabbos goy*"?

Unfortunately, on all these and related issues, halacha is silent today. For the time being, halacha is in exile in the land of Israel as it was before in the lands of Jewish dispersion. It is still the halacha of the *shtetl*, not that of the state. As yet we have not become worthy of the Torah of the land of Israel. The reasons are to be found in what happened to halacha during its exile. Because of the lack of opportunity for halachic application to real-life situations of national existence, the art and wisdom of such application dried up. Because of halacha's exile into literature and codification, new, seemingly insurmountable authority barriers were erected. The old principle of the acceptance of personal responsibility for halachic decisions, which demanded that the *dayan* rule according to what his eyes see,[10] has received a new meaning that reads: according to what he sees in some authoritative text. It was against such an attitude that the warning of R. Abraham the son of Maimonides was directed. Because of its importance, we shall quote it again here:

> The rule of the matter is—say I—that a *dayan* who in his decisions follows only what is written and clearly stated is weak and wanting. Such an attitude invalidates what they [i.e., our sages] said: "A *dayan* has to be guided only by his own understanding." [With him] it is not so. What is written are the roots. Every *dayan* and everyone who renders decisions must weigh them according to each case that comes before him. Every decision [that he is considering] he should compare to something similar to it. He should develop branches from the roots. The numerous case histories in the Talmud, which incorporate only part of the laws, were not reported for nothing; neither were they recorded so that in those matters the law should always be as it is written there. They were preserved only so the wise man, by hearing them often, should acquire efficiency in weighing matters rationally as well as a good method of making decisions.

It is remarkable that such words should come from the son of Maimonides. They imply an unintended criticism of his father's code, which was meant—as we have seen—to replace all other sources of halacha. "Study this and know the law" was the gist of Maimonides' work. In essence, R. Abraham was warning against a new form of Karaism, against becoming Karaites of the written-down Oral Torah. Our present-day halachic authorities have largely succumbed to that danger. After the establishment of the State of Israel, there was a great deal of discussion about the possibility of reestablishing the Sanhedrin as the supreme instance to rule in all matters of halacha in this new era of Jewish national existence. The problem was seen as a halachic one: whether it was justified and possible to renew the institution of *semicha*, the authorization without which no one may become a member of the Sanhedrin. It would seem to us that the entire halachic discussion was pointless at that juncture. The problem is first of all a practical one. The accepted halachic authorities and teachers of today are incapable of functioning in a Sanhedrin. The assembling of seventy-one talmudic scholars, as we know them today, does not make a Sanhedrin.

The Karaite inclination of Torah scholars toward the codified phase of the halacha is also responsible for their estrangement from the realities of Jewish life in the diaspora and even more so in the State of Israel. If one sees the supreme manifestation of halacha in its codified form, his chief preoccupation will be with the text. Too much text may blind us to the realities awaiting the life-giving word of the Torah. And thus, the latter-day Karaite is caught in a vicious circle. Because of his exaggerated bondage to the written word, he becomes alienated from the life within which Torah is to be realized. Because of his alienation from life, he fails to note in his textual studies that the very essence of halacha is its concern with life, the concrete situation in which the Jewish people, as individuals and as a collective, find themselves at any given time.

This twofold alienation, from life and from halacha's concern with it, can be best illustrated by the one-sided educational ideal of the yeshivot in Israel. In general, they frown on secular studies. But a state needs an army, an economic system, health and welfare services, scientific research, technology, etc. The question, therefore, is: Does the Torah desire a Jewish people living in its own land or not? If the answer is affirmative, then the Torah must also desire soldiers, physicians, scientists, architects, engineers, policemen, social workers, etc. To say that these professionals should all come from the secular segment of the population would be a confession that the Torah cannot cope with life. On the other hand, to divide the people into a religious elite, exclusively dedicated to Torah study, and a professional majority, rather ignorant of Torah, incarcerates students of the Torah in another form of a Diaspora Museum, that of the present-day yeshivot.

It is customary for Talmud scholars to refer to their communities as the "yeshiva world." This, of course, is a misnomer. All the yeshivot in the world put together do not make a world. That is the crux of our problem. In a Jewish state, halacha dare not refuse to accept responsibility for the effective functioning of the entire body politic. This requires a new educational philosophy, which in turn would lead to new methods of learning Torah and Talmud and new ways of teaching it.[11]

The new reality of the State of Israel demands an understanding of what halacha is about in its original, classical sense. The Oral Torah has to be freed from its exile-imposed shackles. What was done to it happened, as we have seen, against the directives of the Torah itself. It was done as an act of "disregarding the Torah in order to act for God,"[12] forced upon the Torah by external conditions. Surely this, too, is a time to act for God to restore—as much as possible—the original character of the Oral Torah.

First of all, we have to take to heart the warning of Maimonides' son to treat the numerous codes and other halachic texts not as authority barriers but as educational materials, learning from them the principles and method of Torah application to real-life situations. The decisions have to be made not by a text, but, in full view and understanding of the situation at hand, by the student of the text on his own responsibility. One has to take seriously the admonishment of R. Papa not to waver in accepting responsibility, for the *dayan* is obligated to rule in accordance with his own understanding of the case before him. One dare not relegate responsibility to a text. One must aim at redeeming halacha from its exile from reality by enabling it to encounter the real issues in the life of the Jewish people in this phase of its regained statehood.

The first step in this direction should be a maturing of the understanding that in a state of the Jews, one is dealing not with congregations but with a people. It is relatively easy to manage the congregational structure. Congregations have their declared ideologies. Those who subscribe to them are in; those who do not are out. One may lament the attitude of the outsiders, but one need not be concerned about them very much. A people is always in. Halacha, in its authentic function, must address itself to the Jewish people and not to individuals with sectarian ideologies. To face the people and understand the innate desire of the halacha to address itself to the life of the people in its comprehensive totality may open the door to free the halachic scholar from his Karaitic alienation from reality.

Finally, to help restore the Oral Torah's original status, one has to use the openings distinctly offered by the halacha itself. The Mishna says, as we have seen, that the minority opinion has been recorded so that if a court ever finds this position more valid than that of the majority, it may then overrule the majority, even if it is a lesser court than that of the majority whose opinion has already been accepted as halacha.[13] At this stage, no one can say in how many instances this procedure ought to be followed in order to solve contemporary halachic problems. Adopting this procedure would not mean changing halacha but, on the contrary, following halachic instruction. In fact, in most cases there is no need to change former decisions. The conditions of human existence and the mores of the people have changed radically since the days when the contents of the Oral Torah were poured into vessels of codification. The task is not to change halacha but to apply it to situations to which it has never been applied. We shall mention one or two examples.

Two distinguished talmudic rabbis, Abaye and Rava, discuss who is qualified to testify in a rabbinical court. Abaye maintains that a person who transgresses any of what are usually called ritual commandments is not to be admitted as a witness. For instance, if, out of conviction, as an act of rebellion against the divine commandment, he refuses to observe the dietary laws, he does not qualify as a witness. Rava, on the other hand, asserts that only a person who deals dishonestly with his fellow men is not to be trusted as a witness. In this case, the halacha was decided according to Abaye.[14]

Undoubtedly, this was the correct decision in a society in which living in accordance with the commandments of the Torah was the norm of civilized behavior. One who violated that norm was indeed in most cases not quite trustworthy. Obviously, different conditions prevail today. Can we in all honesty say that a Jew who does not observe the dietary laws is not to be trusted as a witness? We have seen Maimonides explain, in the case of the husband who travels overseas and is never heard of again, why two witnesses are not required. The Torah's interest in them is to establish the facts. If that purpose can be achieved by other means, they may be used, if there is reason for doing so. Similar, and even more decisive in this matter, was the position taken by the teacher of the Ritva.[15] Dare we in good conscience disqualify as witnesses the majority of Jews, who in their interpersonal relationships are no less honest and trustworthy than the Jew who observes the dietary laws? Today, to rule with Rava against Abaye would not be a change of halacha. Abaye never ruled in the situation that obtains today. Let us recall Rava's admonishment to his disciples not to follow his decisions after his death should they disagree with them. What he meant, the commentaries explain, was that had he lived until that day, he might have changed his own opinion.[16]

The problem of autopsies in Israel may serve as another example. In the rather heated discussion of the subject, those who oppose autopsy on halachic grounds rely on the ruling of the Noda Biyhuda, the great R. Yehezkel Landau of Prague. Far be it from us to suggest a halachic solution to the autopsy problem in this study.[17] But obviously R. Landau gave his opinion in the eighteenth century for Jewish communities in exile. The responsibility for medical research and medical services was not upon the Jewish community. This was a typical exile-determined situation. The Noda Biyhuda did not give his ruling in a twentieth-century Jewish state, in which the responsibility for a national health service rests exclusively on the Jewish conscience. No one may say how R. Landau would have ruled in the present situation in Israel. Therefore, should any halachic scholar find sufficient reason to give halachic permission for autopsies in Israel, he would not be opposing the decision of the revered rabbi of Prague.

Let us recall the talmudic saying that "these as well as those are the words of the living God" and Rashi's explanation: "Both opinions are valid, for halachic reasons change even with only small changes in the situation."

One may judge the extent to which halacha is in exile today even in the State of Israel by the way the commandment of the sabbatical year is observed there. The Bible determines that every seventh year in the Jewish calendar be observed as a "Sabbath of the land":

> Six years you shall sow your field, and six years you shall prune your vineyard and gather in the produce thereof. But in the seventh year shall be a Sabbath of solemn rest for the land. A Sabbath unto the Eternal; you shall neither sow your field nor prune your vineyard.[18]

Another law decreed:

> At the end of every seven years you shall make a release. And this is the manner of the release: every creditor shall

release that which he has lent unto his neighbor; he shall not exact it of his neighbor and his brother; because the Eternal's release has been proclaimed.[19]

We have discussed the regulation of the *prozbul*, instituted by Hillel because in his day the law of releasing all debtors from their debts every seventh year had become unworkable.[20] Quite clearly the law of release was intended for a rather primitive agricultural society in which the poor borrowed money for their livelihood to tide them over till the next harvest. In our day, when the entire national economy is based on credit, a law of release would be inconceivable. It would destroy the entire economic structure. Life itself would come to a standstill. As we indicated earlier, changing that law would constitute no real change, because it was never intended for present economic conditions.

Whereas the law of release was a personal obligation incumbent on every Jew wherever he may live, the sabbatical for the land was tied exclusively to the land of Israel. Needless to say, to leave all the land in a Jewish state in the twentieth century untilled every seventh year would spell its destruction. True, the Torah does mention: "And if you will say, 'What shall we eat in the seventh year? Behold we may not sow, nor may we gather in its yield.' I shall command my blessing unto you in the sixth year, and it will produce for three years."[21] Once again, this applies to an agricultural society in which people work the land for their daily food needs. However, this law too is unworkable in a mechanized and industrialized agricultural system; in a society in which the land is tilled not only for domestic consumption but also for export, upon which vital sectors of the national economy depend.

The mutuality of international commercial dependence renders the observance of a Sabbath for the land every seventh year infeasible. This is fully understood by the religious segment of the Israeli population. Two kinds of solutions have been found. The official religious establishment, guided by the chief rabbinate, has accepted the solution proposed by acknowledged rabbinical authorities. It sells Jewish-owned land to Gentiles for the entire sabbatical period with the understanding that the original owners remain on the land as tenants. The Torah does not require that land owned by non-Jews observe the sabbatical year. This solution is based chiefly on the halachic opinion that since the dispersion of the ten tribes from the northern kingdom, the observance of the sabbatical year has ceased to be a biblical commandment and is only a rabbinical injunction. Because of the pressure of circumstances, it is—as is the rule with rabbinical rulings—permissible to circumvent it.

A minority of religious Jews in Israel rejects the official solution. These Jews argue that it is not quite certain from the talmudic sources that sabbatical observance in our days is only a rabbinical obligation. They also question the legal validity of a "sale" of the land, seemingly a tricky evasion of the law. Apart from using hydroponds in a limited sector of their agricultural economy, their solution lies in a "sabbatical fund"—based mainly on diaspora financial contributions—to support agricultural settlements during the land's sabbatical year.

We cannot help seeing both of these solutions as depressing manifestations of exilic halacha in the State of Israel. To refrain from tilling the land and to maintain one's economy through financial support, mainly from non-sabbatical-observing diaspora Jewry, is a confession that, in present conditions, the sabbatical law is unworkable. Surely, it could not have been the intention of the divine lawgiver that the majority of the Jewish people should live in dispersion and the Sabbath of the land be observed through their charitable generosity.

Even more objectionable is the solution of the chief rabbinate. Apart from the very questionable validity of the "sale," is it not self-demeaning to sell the entire agricultural area of the Jewish people in the State of Israel to non-Jews every seventh year—for this is what one would have to do if all Israel were Torah-observant! It is true that great halachic authorities, among them Rabbi Isaac Elhanan Spector of Kovno, suggested this way out. But that was before the establishment of the state. Even the first chief rabbi of the land of Israel, the revered Rabbi Abraham Isaac Kook, of blessed memory, as one of his reasons for the "sale," mentions that "Jewish-owned land in Eretz Yisrael is minimal, and the pressure of circumstances compels us to make use of the permission to sell, since there are grounds to rely on it."[22] But to "sell" the land of Israel every seventh year is a farce that we should have been spared. In our opinion, both these solutions contradict the spirit of the Oral Torah and distort the intention of the sabbatical law.

Let us see how the problem of the sabbatical year was handled in the classical period of the halacha. We are already familiar with the difficulties the people faced under the Roman occupation of the land of Israel. A yearly tax had to be delivered to the authorities from the produce of the land. R. Yanai therefore announced to the people: "Go out and sow the land in the sabbatical year because of the tax."[23] Rashi explains that R. Yanai could make such an announcement because "in this time" the sabbatical year was only a rabbinical law, but from Rashi's style it is clear that he himself is of the opinion that this holds true today as well.

For our understanding of our contemporary problem, it is even more important to consider the interpretation of Tosafot that claims that R. Yanai's proclamation could be made even on the basis of the opinion that the sabbatical year remains a biblical command for all times. Quoting from the story as told in the Jerusalem Talmud, Tosafot believe there could have been a danger to life if the tax had not been paid.[24] It is, of course, a generally valid halachic principle that (with only three exceptions) no law in the Torah is obligatory where its observance may endanger life. In other words, the non-observance of a biblical command in such cases is not a violation but, on the contrary, the observance of a supervening law that protects life.[25] Surely, this is the principle by which the problem of sabbatical observance in a modern Jewish state should be approached.

It may be helpful to pay attention to how R. Yehuda Hanasi, the editor of the Mishna, contended with the problem of the sabbatical year. He eliminated one area after another from the boundaries of the land within which the sabbatical had to be observed.[26] When he had exempted the entire area of Beit She'an too from sabbatical observance, the Talmud tells us, his brothers and the whole house of his father joined forces against him, saying: "A place that your fathers and fathers' fathers treated as forbidden [for work in the sabbatical year] you treat as permitted?!" R. Yehuda answered them with a midrash of his own making. Of King Hezekiah it is told in the Bible: "And he broke in pieces the brazen serpent that Moses had made;[27] for unto those days the children of Israel did offer to it; and it was called Nehushtan."[28] Explained R. Yehuda: "How was it possible that

Asa had come and did not destroy it, then Jehoshaphat, and did not destroy it either? These two kings had destroyed all the idols in their time. But his forefathers left Hezekiah an opportunity to prove himself. Thus, in my case too, my ancestors left me this opportunity to prove myself."[29] In fact, R. Yehuda was saying to his brothers and to the entire house of his fathers: "This has now become my problem; it is my duty to solve it."

What motivated R. Yehuda to exempt as many districts as possible from the commandment of the sabbatical year? It may be learned from the Jerusalem Talmud. It used to be customary to declare a public fast, as a form of repentance and supplication, whenever danger threatened the community. Such a fast was declared in times of drought or when disease befell the crops. "It was taught: Just as one proclaims these fasts in other years, one does so in the sabbatical year too." This, of course, requires a reason. Why should one fast and pray for rain in a sabbatical year, when in any case we must not till the land? "We do it," says the Talmud, "for the sustenance of others."

Who are the "others"? The Talmud quotes two interpretations. One is that the others are the Gentiles. They need not observe the sabbatical year in the land of Israel, so we institute a public fast asking for rain in their fields. This seems to be the view of the majority. R. Zeira, however, said that the "others" are the Jews suspected of not observing the sabbatical year. They work their fields, and their fields need rain. What does this mean? A public fast for the sake of transgressors of a biblical law?! The answer is given that R. Zeira follows the teaching of R. Yehuda Hanasi. And then a story is told. There was a man suspected of violating the sabbatical commandment. They brought him before R. Yehuda. He said to them: "What should this poor man do? He works [his land] in order to keep himself alive."[30]

Actually, Rabbenu Hakadosh once abolished sabbatical observance completely. He did so because he reasoned that the law no longer applied, that it was only a rabbinical injunction, lest the idea of the sabbatical year be forgotten. Therefore, because of economic need, he felt justified in disregarding a rabbinical institution. This is a generally followed halachic principle. However, his ruling in this matter was rejected. R. Pinhas ben Yair opposed it, not in an open discussion of views but—significantly—in a private, non-halachic conversation in which he hinted to R. Yehuda that his abolishment of the sabbatical year was not being followed.[31]

What was the difference between R. Yehuda Hanasi and R. Pinhas ben Yair? R. Pinhas ben Yair led a saintly life of such intensity that, according to talmudic lore, even his donkey would not touch untithed food. But he was a private person, without any responsibility of office. R. Yehuda, the head of the Sanhedrin, was responsible for the well-being of his people, socially and economically. From the story about the poor man who tilled his field in the sabbatical year, we may conclude that even after the rejection of his general abolition of the sabbatical practice, R. Yehuda insisted on exemptions for the needy. One wonders whether it is just a coincidence that the Jerusalem Talmud—taught in the land of Israel, where the sabbatical law originally applied—maintains that the sabbatical year in our time is no longer a biblical commandment, whereas the Babylonian Talmud, the work of Babylonian Jewry, for whom the sabbatical year was never obligatory, allows a disagreement between the sages on the subject.[32] It is not our intention to give any halachic rulings in this study. One cannot help wondering what R. Pinhas ben Yair's stand would have been had he been confronted with the problem of sabbatical observance in a Jewish state in the twentieth century.

The sabbatical year expresses an important ideal of Torah teaching. The very language used by the Bible, that "the land rest," speaks of a relationship between nature and man from which modern man in an industrialized society has become dangerously alienated. The "great Sabbath" (*shabbat shabbaton*) that the land should observe as a "Sabbath unto God"—a phrasing very similar to the one used for Sabbath observance by man—suggests an intimate God-nature relationship that limits man's proprietorship over the land. The sabbatical year frees the land from total human ownership. The yield of the land in that year, whatever grows without human effort, is ownerless and available for all, including the animals of the earth. The philosophy of the interrelatedness of all life within itself and with its Creator is the seed of vital ecological and socioethical insights, responsibility, and promise. Whatever solution may be found for the sabbatical problem of our own day, the sabbatical ideal should be not only preserved but also implemented.

FROM AN AGENDA FOR HALACHA

One of the most disturbing issues in the area of halacha that requires immediate and courageous attention is the status of the woman. A careful student cannot but admire the intellectual honesty with which the teachers of the Talmud and Midrash occasionally express themselves in their discussion of biblical laws. One of the most surprising examples is their understanding of the disadvantaged legal status of the woman. Following the Bible, the Promised Land was to be distributed among the tribes of the children of Israel to the males of each family. Zelophehad, who had been put to death, had left no sons, only daughters. Was the family to be excluded from a share in the land? Zelophehad's daughters approached Moses. *Sifrei* comments on their case:

> When the daughters of Zelophehad heard that the land was to be parceled out only to the male and not the female members of the tribes, they met to take counsel together. They said: "The loving-kindness of those of flesh and blood is not like that of God. Flesh and blood's loving-kindness discriminates, preferring males to females; the loving-kindness of God is bestowed equally on both, for it is written, 'God is good to all; his loving-kindness is upon all his works.'"[33]

Moses took the plea of the daughters to God himself, and arrangements were made for families without sons. But what does this midrash suggest? It seems to say that even though the Torah is from heaven, the legal inequality between man and woman is not God's doing but man's. According to our understanding, this midrash implies that in questions pertaining to the legal status of the woman, the words of the psalmist—"God is good to all; his loving-kindness is upon all his works"—must guide the halachic application of Torah to life. God himself gave the direction in the case of Zelophehad's daughters. Of course, the principle was applied only to the case at hand. But as we saw above, did not R. Yehuda explain that his ancestors left him an opportunity to prove himself? Each generation has its own problems and its own obligation to accept responsibility.

We have seen how the teachers of the talmudic and later periods met the halachic challenges of their times. The *ketuba* was instituted to discourage a man from sending his wife away at every whim. In cases when a woman could not be expected to remain married to her husband, he was compelled to divorce his wife "freely." Even when a woman requested a divorce on the grounds of incompatibility (the "rebellious woman"), some of the leading authorities ruled that the husband had to give her a *get*. Even those who did not find this opinion well grounded in talmudic sources introduced their own *takana* to that end. To protect a woman from becoming an *aguna*, ways were found to admit testimony that normally would have no validity. In certain cases a marriage could be annulled retroactively, or a biblical law could simply be disregarded because the husband had espoused his wife in an objectionable manner. A quarreling husband or one who beat his wife was warned twice by the rabbinical court to desist. If the warnings did not help, he was forced to divorce her by his "free will."[34] After the redaction of the Talmud, numerous other *takanot* protected the interests of the wife.

Rabbenu Asher (Rosh), the father of the author of the *Turim*, said of the *herem* of Rabbenu Gershon, which forbade a husband to divorce his wife against her will, that it established equality between husband and wife. Just as a husband was not to be forced to divorce his wife against his will, neither could she now be divorced against her will. Undoubtedly, Rosh was right. The *herem* of Rabbenu Gershon was a great improvement in the status of women, meeting some urgent problems of his day. However, things have changed greatly since the tenth century. No one could say today that, according to the present-day administration of halacha, husband and wife have equal rights. Yet the daughters of Zelophehad were correct in asking for such equality in the name of God, who "is good to all [and whose] loving-kindness is upon all his works." We shall limit our discussion here to the subject of marriage law.

The problem of the *aguna* has occupied the teachers of halacha since the earliest days. A talmudic tradition has it that the men who went to war in the days of King David each gave their wives a *get*, the divorce to take effect retroactively in case they did not return from battle. Thus, the wives were protected from becoming *agunot*.[35] In our own day the problem exists in a different form even in times of peace. In the diaspora, marriages are dissolved in civil courts in accordance with the law of the country. This, of course, is not enough to bring about a divorce in a marriage concluded "according to the laws of Moses and Israel." Only a *get* handed to the woman can effect a Jewish divorce. But as things stand today, if the husband refuses to give a *get*, the wife has no recourse to any authority.

The consequences are extremely serious. From a purely religious point of view, if the husband remarries after a civil divorce, he has only transgressed the injunction of Rabbenu Gershon against polygamy, which is not forbidden by biblical law. But should the wife remarry without having obtained a *get*, she commits adultery, and her children by her civil-law husband are *mamzerim*. From an exclusively ethical point of view, the situation is no less serious. At times, after the marriage has been dissolved by the civil authorities, a husband will refuse his wife the *get* as an act of revenge; or an unscrupulous husband will use his power for purposes of extortion, blackmailing his wife and her family. There is probably hardly a congregational rabbi who has not come across such a situation.

The consequence of the insanity of one of the marriage partners is another example of inequality between husband and wife. If the wife becomes mentally incapacitated, she cannot be divorced, but—even in countries where the *herem* of Rabbenu Gershon against polygamy is accepted—the husband may get a dispensation from the *herem* to marry another woman. But if the husband becomes insane, there is no way of arranging a divorce for the wife. This may have especially cruel consequences if the husband did not inform his wife prior to their marriage that he had previously endured fits of mental disorder. Many are the human tragedies for which the administration of this law is responsible.

Most incongruous is the way the laws of levirate marriage are implemented. Already in mishnaic times, as we have seen, the implementation of this law presented serious practical difficulties.[36] The marriage had to be undertaken with the intention of fulfilling a *mitzva*. If the couple married for purely personal reasons—because they loved each other, or because the woman sought economic security or social status, or because the brother-in-law wanted to inherit the property of his dead brother—not only did they not fulfill the levirate commandment, but they actually violated the prohibition of marrying the wife of one's brother. Thus, levirate marriage was discouraged; according to one opinion, it was even forbidden. The *halitza* ceremony took its place, by which the widow was freed to marry outside the family of her late husband. Finally, it was resolved that only in exceptional situations was *yibum* permitted, and only when both the widow and the brother-in-law wished to marry solely to fulfill the *mitzva* prescribed in the Torah.[37] Thus, as a rule, in accordance with the biblical provision, *halitza* replaced levirate marriage. For the *halitza* ceremony, the widow

and the brother-in-law appear before the rabbinical court, where
she declares:

> "My husband's brother refuses to raise up unto his brother
> a name in Israel; he will not perform the duty of a hus-
> band's brother unto me." Upon which the brother-in-law
> says: "I do not want to take her"; then shall his brother's
> wife draw nigh unto him in the presence of the elders and
> loose his shoe from off his foot and spit in his face; and
> she shall answer and say: "So shall it be done unto the man
> who does not build up his brother's house." And his name
> shall be called in Israel, "The house of him who had his shoe
> loosed."[38]

In truth, both *yibum* and *halitza* were extremely important
institutions in a rather primitive agricultural and tribal society.
Today, however, the social and economic basis of this law has
disappeared. It is doubtful that either levirate marriage or *halitza*
can have any meaning even for many Orthodox Jews. Furthermore, under the present circumstances, the *halitza* ceremony
seems unfair to the brother-in-law. It is not that he does not
wish to marry the widow, but that he is discouraged, and mostly
prevented, from marrying her by the halacha. Even if he wanted
to marry her only in order to fulfill the biblical commandment,
he would have to undergo the humiliating ceremony of *halitza*
if the widow couldn't marry him for such a lofty purpose. Moreover, since a Torah-observant woman cannot remarry without
performing the *halitza* act, she often becomes the target of
blackmail by an unscrupulous brother-in-law, who might think
it only right that he too should share in his brother's estate.

Other problems await solutions. The responsa literature
throughout the ages is filled with cases of women whose lives

became sheer misery because of beatings by their husbands or because of the continuous quarrels and mistreatments to which they were subjected. Some authorities rule that unless the husband reforms, we compel him to divorce his wife.[39] That is how the law is recorded in *Shulhan Aruch*: If after two warnings he does not change his ways, he must give his wife a *get*.

In the diaspora, the rabbinate lacks the power to impose this law of the *Shulhan Aruch* on a recalcitrant husband. Even in Israel, tragically, the rabbinate is largely insensitive to the problem. Many cases of wife-beating and other mistreatment remain in the courts for years without a resolution. The rabbinate in Israel does not make use of the opportunities provided for in the halacha itself. Neither has any progress been made in all the other thorny areas presented here. True, the complications caused by civil divorce in the diaspora do not exist in the State of Israel. But even in Israel, apart from husbands missing in a war, there are always numerous cases of husbands who leave the country without divorcing their wives and agree to send a *get* only in return for exorbitant financial compensation.

Ethically, the situation is hardly bearable, especially in times of national crisis. Let two personal experiences speak here for innumerable others. Toward the end of 1938 and early in 1939, there was a case in Berlin of a young woman whose husband was in a mental asylum. Every Jew was trying to get out of Germany. Thus, the woman sought a rabbinical court to arrange a divorce for her, so she could save herself and her five-year-old child. She would not have been leaving her husband in the lurch. She had every moral reason to demand a divorce: Prior to their marriage, he had contracted syphilis. He did not have it treated. By the time of their marriage the sickness had reached a stage when it was no longer contagious. The man married without informing his bride of the condition of his health. As the years passed, the disease attacked his brain and he became insane. As indicated earlier, an insane person is not competent to authorize the writing and transfer of the divorce document.

The poor woman was running from rabbi to rabbi in Berlin to no avail. No one wanted to touch her case. Finally, someone advised her to seek me out. I was then the youngest rabbi serving the Jewish community, still in my twenties. The first question I asked myself was: Is the halachic concept of incompetence due to insanity identical with the medical definition? I visited the man in the asylum and concluded that, from a halachic point of view, he was quite capable of giving a *get*. Consequently, I wrote a responsum about the case, proving that halachically the husband was competent. I submitted it to Rabbi Yehiel Jacob Weinberg, of blessed memory, the internationally recognized halachic authority. On his visit to Vilna, he discussed the matter with the venerable Rabbi Hayim Ozer Grodzinski, of blessed memory, and came back with the message that the latter agreed with my findings. (R. Weinberg published my responsum in his work *S'ridei Esh*, vol. 3, 35.)[40]

Unfortunately, I was unable to bring the matter to a successful conclusion. First of all, the husband understood the meaning of a *get* so well that he refused to cooperate. Possibly, this difficulty could have been overcome. The technical difficulties were insurmountable—so I felt. One would have had to bring a scribe to the asylum, so the husband could personally authorize him to write the *get*. In addition, two witnesses would have had to be present, and a messenger would have to be authorized by the husband to hand the *get* to his wife. I felt unable to move the Nazi hospital authorities to help in the matter.

Eventually, my family and I left Germany, but what became of the poor woman and her child? And yet, all this was unnecessary. It could have been easily prevented. Had I, in those early years of my rabbinical career, had the experience and halachic understanding I acquired later, I would have made the case for annulling her marriage retroactively, because the husband had failed to inform her about the state of his health. It would have been relatively easy, under the prevailing conditions, to give the ruling a solid halachic foundation.

No one knows how many problems arose from similar or related situations, and how much human suffering, in the years soon after the European tragedy of the Jewish people. Let one post-Holocaust personal experience—much less tragic but morally quite disturbing—illustrate the point. I was a rabbi in Sydney, Australia. One day, a couple came to my office. The woman was a concentration-camp survivor. She had lost everything. Her entire family had been wiped out. She had been married but had no children. Her husband, too, had been murdered. She was alone in the world. Through correspondence she had discovered that a friend of hers from her hometown had managed to get to Australia. She came to Australia to marry him. But... her late husband once had a brother. What had become of him, no one knew. Was he alive somewhere, or had he too been murdered? If he was still alive, the woman needed *halitza* before she could remarry.

What was the rabbi to do? Institute an international search for witnesses? And in the meantime? Hadn't she suffered enough, not a personal fate but the fate of all Israel? Finally she had found someone willing to build a new home with her, to start a new life. What was to be her situation in the meantime, till all the inquiries were made and all the answers received? What if a brother-in-law were found alive in some distant land? Establish contact with him. Would he be willing or able to come to Australia for the *halitza*, or would she have to leave the promised shores of her hope in order to participate in the ceremony? Meanwhile, would she have to be placed in some kind of halachic quarantine, remaining homeless and awaiting happiness? By God, this was not what the Torah meant! This was not halacha; certainly not "ways of pleasantness and paths of peace"!

The tragic aspect of the present situation is that all the problems we have discussed in this section, and related ones, can be solved. In my halachic work *Conditionality in Marriage and Divorce*, I have shown that by including proper safeguards in the terms of the marriage contract, such predicaments can be eliminated *ab initio*. The practice of our time in the application of the Torah's marriage and divorce laws often leads to grievous human suffering and much desecration of God's name. It is ethically indefensible; but halacha is not responsible for it.

One of the most serious problems of our day is the widespread ideological fragmentation within the Jewish people. The religious ideologies are numerous. Yet Judaism in its very essence is not sectarian but the way of life *of* a people. Indeed, it can be fully realized only by a people. To work for Jewish unity in the spirit of *ahavat Yisrael*, love for every Jew, in the interest of *klal Yisrael*, the reality of the totality of the Jewish people, is an urgent demand of Torah realization. Regrettably, rather than contributing to the striving for Jewish unity, halacha as understood today only deepens and fortifies the fragmentation. As a matter of principle, the Orthodox establishment refuses to grant recognition in matters concerning halacha to representatives of other ideological groupings within Judaism. This monopoly finds expression especially in the area of marriage and divorce as well as in that of conversion. In Israel, non-Orthodox rabbis are not permitted by the law of the state to perform any functions in those fields; in the diaspora, their activities therein are usually dismissed as having no halachic validity.

It is our conviction that halacha must be stretched to its limits in order to further Jewish unity and mutual understanding. In the Orthodox camp, certain psychological impediments have to be overcome. It is time that Orthodox rabbis face without dogmatism the issue of their relationship to rabbis of the non-Orthodox denominations. It is just not true that the latter, because of their Conservative or Reform interpretation of Judaism, are incapable of fear of Heaven. To insist otherwise is a prejudice; it is insisting on an untruth that, as such, is a violation of important biblical commandments. There are quite a few among Conservative and Reform rabbis who are sincere believers in Judaism.

Nor should it be taken for granted that belonging to the Orthodox group automatically bestows upon one the precious treasure of fear of Heaven. True, some practices and teachings of non-Orthodox rabbis violate the laws of the Torah as understood by Orthodox interpretation. But it is not true that these rabbis interpret and practice as they do because they mean to perform an act of heresy or rebellion against Judaism. On the contrary, many among them work to preserve, to enrich, to serve Judaism and the Jewish people no less than the best of their Orthodox colleagues. Ideologically, their intention may be no less for the sake of Heaven than that of Orthodox Jews.

What is their halachic status? Since they do violate the law not with the knowledge or intention of violating but, on the contrary, with the conviction—however mistaken from the Orthodox point of view—of practicing a valid form of Judaism, they are not to be considered *mumrim l'hachis*, apostates out of spite or even *mumrim l'teavon*, apostates of convenience. From the halachic point of view, they are *toim*, simply mistaken.[41] This description should not be taken as a form of condescension. We are attempting to define their status from the point of view of halacha. I fully realize that non-Orthodox interpreters of Judaism may similarly refer to the Orthodox interpretation as mistaken. Ideological differences should not be watered down, but neither should they destroy the respect we owe each other, nor should they erode our sense of responsibility to work for unity in Israel to the ultimate limit that our ideological positions permit.

The question, of course, is: What are those limits? Let us, as an example, consider the issue of conversion. Once again, we have before us a conflict between specific laws and one comprehensive Torah obligation. The specific laws are those of conversion; the comprehensive obligation is the commandment to love every Jew and work for peace and unity. I have suggested that in this encounter between commandment and commandment, the more comprehensive obligation creates a condition of *sha'at hadhak* and *tzorech gadol*, a time of urgency and great need.[42] Halachically, we distinguish between what a law requires *a priori*, as the direct, initial command, and what is acceptable after the fact, once something has been done not quite in complete adherence to the law. Another halachic principle provides that whatever is allowed after the fact is permitted even initially at a time of "urgency and great need." These tenets indicate the extent to which the halacha may guide us in pursuing peace and a measure of cooperation between the various religious denominations among us. We shall attempt to formulate some of these ideas. We intend to illustrate our meaning at some length by discussing the issue of conversion in the light of our suggestion.

What are the halachic requirements for the conversion of a Gentile to Judaism?

1. The conversion has to be sincere; Judaism must be accepted out of conviction, for its own sake, and without ulterior considerations.

2. It must imply the "acceptance of commandments"; in the case of a male, circumcision, and in all cases immersion in a *mikveh* (ritual bath).

3. It has to take place before a *beit din*, a "court of law," consisting of three members.

4. The court must carefully examine the motives of the would-be convert. For this purpose, the "convert" is at first to be discouraged by explaining to him the hardships of being a Jew in a generally unfriendly world. If he insists, and the sincerity of his motives has been established, one informs him of some of the easier as well as some of the more difficult commandments of the Torah and explains to him their significance in general terms. If he is undeterred, one proceeds in an encouraging manner, drawing him near to the truth of Judaism. Finally, the conversion is concluded by circumcision and immersion in the *mikveh* as stipulated in the Talmud and the codes.

However, these requirements need some explanation as well as qualification.

Though sincerity of motivation is required *a priori*, if one accepts Judaism for reasons of marriage or for some other ulterior motive, he is accepted as a Jew.[43] Of course, even in such cases, there has to be formal acceptance of Judaism.

More important, however, is the qualification that the "sincerity of motivation" is not to be interpreted strictly. There is the story of the Gentile who came to Hillel to be converted on condition that he would be appointed a high priest.[44] Or the case of the woman who asked R. Hiya to be converted in order to be able to marry one of his disciples.[45] Both were converted. The generally accepted explanation is the one given by Tosafot that both rabbis were sure that the Gentile involved would ultimately, after the actual conversion, practice Judaism for the sake of Heaven. In other words, the sincerity of these converts was judged not purely on the grounds of their momentary, consciously realized motivation, but on its expected outcome. This is a matter to be evaluated in light of the character of the people involved and the specific situation in which they decide to convert.

There is no reason to assume that such insight into the future development of a convert's relationship to Judaism is granted only to a Hillel or a R. Hiya. And, indeed, *Beit Yosef* derives from these stories the principle that "everything depends on the judgment of the court," or on its appreciation of where this kind of conversion for some ulterior motive will ultimately lead.[46] What these stories and the interpretation of them mean is that there is no hard and fast rule in these matters. At times, it is proper to discourage initially; at other times, one should be helpful right at the outset. Indeed, the Talmud tells the story of Timna, the concubine of Eliphaz the son of Esau, who wanted to be converted but was rejected by Abraham, Isaac, and Jacob. The result was that Amalek, the classical enemy of the Jews, was her offspring. Why did this happen? Answers the Talmud: "They should not have pushed her away."[47]

"Acceptance of commandments" is a *conditio sine qua non*. There can be no conversion without it. But nowhere is it spelled out clearly what is meant by the "acceptance of commandments." The very term is rather vague. Quite clearly it does not mean the acceptance of all the commandments of the Torah. That the court, as the Talmud states, has to inform the convert of "some of the easier *mitzvot* and some of the more difficult ones" proves that it is not even necessary to make known to him all the commandments, which, of course, would be extremely difficult from a practical point of view. But the term "some of the commandments" is also extremely vague. Which commandments? How many of them? Some of them are mentioned in the Talmud.[48] But on the whole, once again the judgment is left to the court.

Does "acceptance of commandments," then, mean the acceptance of the commandments which are made known to the would-be convert?

It is not difficult to show that "acceptance of commandments" is not identical to accepting "some of the easier *mitzvot* and some of the more difficult ones" that the court should make known to the convert. "Acceptance of commandments" is a condition that cannot be waived. Yet Maimonides rules that if a court of laymen neglected to inform the convert of "some of the easier and some of the more difficult commandments," the conversion is valid, if he was circumcised and immersed in the *mikveh*.[49] But there must have been acceptance of command-ments. *Shulhan Aruch* too brings the rule that this acceptance is essential; nevertheless, the author quotes the above decision of Maimonides.[50] The other halachic authorities agree with this ruling.

What then is meant by "acceptance of commandments"? What commandments *have* to be accepted? The only ones left outside "some of the easier and some of the more difficult commandments" are faith in the One God of Israel and the com-mandments of circumcision and immersion in a *mikveh*. The three together represent the entry into the community of Israel. So it would also appear from a passage in tractate Kidushin.[51] Among the various classes of people who left Babylon with Ezra, converts, too, are mentioned. The Talmud asks: How do we know converts were among them? And the answer is given: For it is written, "and all such as had separated themselves unto them from the filthiness of the nations of the land" (the verse continues: "to seek the Eternal, the God of Israel," Ezra 6:21). Converts are identified as people who give up their religion and join the Jewish people to seek the Eternal, the God of Israel. Since these people partook of the paschal lamb together with all the Jews, there must have been circumcision and immersion. Indeed, the phrase "separated themselves unto them" means: renouncing a former faith, accepting faith in the One God of Israel, and joining the people of Israel through the acts of cir-cumcision and immersion.

It would seem to us—and it is possible to show support for this idea in the talmudic sources—that the abjuring of a former religion, the acceptance of faith in the One God of Israel, and the joining of the Jewish people are, of necessity, essential in the intention of becoming a convert and are to be so understood by all who are moved to convert.

But even in informing the convert of some of the *mitzvot*, relatively little is, and can be, made known of the entire, complex teaching of Judaism and the life it demands. Since "acceptance of mitzvot" alone suffices after the fact and is realized by the abjuring of the former faith, the acceptance of faith in the One God of Israel, and circumcision and immersion, it is obviously only a beginning. At this stage the convert cannot have an adequate knowledge of his new faith; he cannot fully realize all the implications of his decision. He has only a general idea of what it means to be a Jew and the willingness to be one. To paraphrase the words of the book of Ezra, conversion means separating oneself from an old faith and joining the Jewish people in order to seek out the God of Israel. In fact, every conversion is similar to that administered by Hillel. An introduction is provided to what is meant by being a Jew. The "rest"—and that is the greatest part of being a Jew, and is probably limitless—is "explanation." Go learn and find out.

What constitutes a *beit din* for conversion? The *Tur* mentions "three talmudic scholars." *Shulhan Aruch* uses the phrase "three who are qualified to judge." At the same time, in ruling about the convert whose reason for conversion was not examined and to whom the commandments were not made known, Maimonides writes: "If he was circumcised and immersed before three laymen, he is a convert." Now, of course, since the cessation of *semicha* (rabbinic ordination), all courts are made up of "laymen" who are scholars.[52] Yet quite clearly Maimonides uses the term here in the sense of "laymen" to whom the adjectives "studied and understand"[53] do not apply. For he wishes to explain why this convert had not been initially examined, why he was not advised about the commandments that would be obligatory upon him as a Jew. These requirements were overlooked because the conversion was administered not by professional judges but by laymen who were ignorant of those requirements. It is noteworthy that whereas Maimonides uses the term *beit din* when he states the requirement for a court, he does not mention that term at all when he rules on what is acceptable *post factum* and says simply: "in the presence of three laymen." In other words, initially a court of talmudic scholars is required, but after the fact three laymen form the "court."

R. Isaac Alfasi is of the opinion that a court of three is needed only *a priori*, but if a conversion took place without a court, it is still valid. Therefore, if such a convert got married, his children are Jews, but if he wishes to get married, it is required that there be immersion in the presence of a court, the idea being that before marriage, the case should be judged as an *a priori* situation and immersion before a court required. At the same time, should he espouse a wife without this second immersion, before a *beit din*, the woman becomes his wife according to the law.[54] Obviously, Alfasi does not consider the requirement of a court a biblical commandment. For him, the verses quoted in the Talmud as the sources for this requirement are an *asmachta*, a mere supporting hint. The commandment is not biblical, and it is therefore not binding *post factum*.

We do not wish to maintain that our discussion of the laws of conversion is already the solution to the problem of disunity. We have intended to show by this example that within halacha there are possibilities for an approach between the various ideological groupings within the Jewish people. Whatever our theological differences, the responsibility to strive for unity in the spirit of loving every Jew is equally binding on all of us. If, from the halachic point of view, the supervening importance of that obligation renders the task one of "urgency and great need," in which the fulfillment of specific laws may be allowed even in their *post factum* form, the same approach to the task of unity may well be demanded of all denominations in our midst. One might ask the teachers of Reform and Conservatism: What is your *post factum*? How far are you willing to go in giving up your ideal form of practice in specific cases for the sake of the comprehensive *mitzva* of Jewish unity?

Needless to say, the problems are very similar in the area of the marriage and divorce laws. Far be it from us to suggest that every marriage ceremony performed by Reform or Conservative rabbis is halachically valid. But neither should one generalize and deem all such marriages halachically invalid. In fact, a halachic authority who gave such a ruling might in numerous cases be responsible for serious transgressions of halacha. Such a decision would actually mean that every couple at whose marriage a Reform or Conservative rabbi officiated is not to be considered married according to Jewish law, and therefore this man and woman may at any time dissolve their union. The woman would then be free to marry whomever she pleased without the halachically prescribed divorce by a *get*. It would be very easy to argue that this would often mean that a married woman could marry another man. In fact, she would be committing adultery.[55]

Once again we confront a conflict between the comprehensive halachic requirement of seeking ways of peace and understanding that further the unity of the Jewish people and the specific laws of halachic marriage and divorce. In this case, too, as in the matter of conversion, halacha is quite capable of providing a basis for responsible dialogue between the various ideological groupings within our people.

CHAPTER FIVE

Halacha in a
Democratic Society

Can halacha function in a democratic society? At this stage in history the answer has to be negative: not as a law obligatory on all. This seems self-evident. Decisions regarding the management of affairs in a democratic society are reached by majority decision. Is it imaginable that a halachic issue be resolved by such a majority vote? Yet a great many democratic elements are incorporated in halacha. Halachic decisions in the Sanhedrin were based on a majority vote, a practice followed to this day in rabbinical courts. As for freedom of speech, of expressing one's opinion on any issue, we have seen that even after the highest court, the Sanhedrin in the Temple, had given its verdict, the "rebellious elder" was permitted to return to his hometown and teach his views in disagreement with the official ruling, though he was not permitted to act against that ruling or to teach others to do so. This would have been breaking the law, which is not tolerated in a democratic society either.

One might, of course, argue that in a democracy every citizen has the right to express an opinion and to vote, whereas in

a Torah society the principle of ruling in accordance with the
majority obtains only in the Sanhedrin or a *beit din*, In a Sanhedrin or a *beit din*, only qualified members have a vote, not
the people. However, even in a democracy, only members of the
court may vote on judicial matters, and only members of the
legislature—of the Senate and the House of Representatives, for
instance, in the United States—have the right to vote in making
laws and in regard to many other important public issues.

It is true that senators and congressmen are elected by the
people, and that judges, when they are appointed, are appointed
by the representatives of the people who invest them with that
kind of executive authority. But neither is this very much different within the system of halacha. Maimonides describes the
manner in which members of the Sanhedrin and other rabbinical courts were appointed. "It is a commandment of the Torah
to appoint judges and officers in all provinces and in all districts,
for it is written: 'Judges and officers you shall give to yourself in
all your gates.'"[1]

This is not the place to discuss the process in detail. In the
final analysis, it is the people who set up the Sanhedrin and
the other courts. These institutions function because they are
accepted by the people. To this day a rabbi has to be elected by
the community, and no matter how great a scholar he may be in
Talmud and halacha, he has authority only in the community in
which he was elected.[2] Perhaps we might argue as follows: It may
be true that the halachic way of setting up a Sanhedrin and a *beit
din* is not essentially different from the democratic process of
electing representatives of the people. But there is a fundamental
difference in the two systems. In a democracy the people's representatives frame the laws by which a given society desires to live,

laws which are then administered by the executive and judiciary branches of the government. For halacha, however, the law
as such was revealed by God at Sinai. The people appoint judges
and officers to administer a system of law over which they have
no control, on whose formulation the people's representatives
have no right to vote; a law that is unchangeable.

It is not quite that simple. No one forced the people to
accept the law from Sinai. The Talmud itself expresses this idea.
According to a midrashic interpretation of some words in the
biblical text that describe the children of Israel's stand at Sinai,
God lifted up the mountain, held it over them all like a trough,
and said: "If you accept the Torah, good. If not, there you will
find your graves!"

This, of course, was compulsion. Indeed, the Talmud continues: "There is reason here to protest against the Torah." One
commentator explains: "If Jews do not observe the commandments, they can always plead that they never agreed to accept the
Torah freely; the Torah was forced upon them." Finally, Rabba
resolves the issue by proving with another midrashic explanation that ultimately, in the days of Ahasuerus, they accepted it
in an act of free choice.[3]

Beyond the midrashic style, what is being stated in this discussion is the idea that even the Torah from Sinai must be freely
accepted. This requirement has remained in place throughout
history. The Jewish people was never compelled to accept the
Torah. The Jews have followed it because they accepted it. The
people acknowledged the Torah; on that basis they determined
who should teach and administer its laws; these functionar-
ies then made their decisions by majority rule. (To prevent the
exertion of authoritative pressure by the head of the Sanhedrin

and the senior members of the court, the discussion and voting proceeded from the youngest and least prestigious members to more respected ones, until it reached the chief justice and finally the president, who was the last to state his opinion and to cast his vote.)

As we have also learned, the people were called into partnership with the word from Sinai in the covenant concluded between them and the Revealer of the word, on the foundations of the Oral Torah. The Torah of the living word freed them from every bondage to fundamentalism. This explains the audacity of R. Yehoshua, who, defying the heavenly voice, declared: "The Torah is no longer in heaven. In agreement with the desire of the Torah, we follow the majority down here."[4]

We shall illustrate our point with a quotation from Maimonides—we are already familiar with it from a previous part of our study—that caused some difficulty for the commentators.[5] Following the Talmud, as is his method, Maimonides laid down the rule:

> Assuming that [the judges of] the great *beit din* [i.e., the Sanhedrin of the Temple Mount], following the rules of Torah interpretation, decided upon a law as it appeared to them to be right: If after them another *beit din* arises that has reason to reject that decision, it has the authority to do so and to rule as it appears correct in its own eyes. For the Bible says: "to the judge who will be in those days"; you are obligated to go only to the judge of your own generation.

R. Joseph Karo, commenting on the work of Maimonides, rightly asks: If so, why are the later rabbis of the Talmud not allowed to disagree with the early ones? Often we find that the Talmud attempts to reject the opinion of a later sage by a quotation from a mishna or another source from the mishnaic period. Usually the answer is then given that the view of that later sage is supported by an earlier one. According to Maimonides, why should a later generation of teachers not be able to disagree with a previous one? However, R. Karo's question should have been directed not against Maimonides but against the passage in the Talmud upon which his formulation is based. Karo explains the matter by saying: "*Maybe* since the day of the conclusion of the Mishna, they resolved and practiced that the later generations were not to disagree with the earlier ones. And so they did also at the conclusion of the Talmud, such that from then on no one had the right to disagree with it."[6]

R. Yosef Karo is not quite sure whether his explanation is indeed the right one. Furthermore, these resolutions and practices were contrary to a halachic principle based on a verse in the Bible. If the Bible tells us that one has to be guided only by the rulings of a contemporary halachic authority, that has vital halachic implications. The reasons for the resolve not to abide by that biblical rule must have been compelling.[7] It is, however, important to realize that this setting aside of a law of the Torah was done by the will of the people. It had validity because the people acknowledged it and abided by it. One may ask why a decision of the people at the time of the conclusion of the Mishna should bind all later generations. Of course, no one generation has the authority to impose such obligations on future generations. The obligation became binding because each generation of Jews who lived by the laws of the Torah and in accordance with halacha adhered to it by their own free will.

All this seems in no way to contradict democratic procedure. Judaism presupposes a society that accepts the Torah freely and lives by the discipline of halacha. But let us assume the existence of a society that has subscribed to the faith in "Torah from Sinai" by a majority vote. What of the dissenting minority? What would be the position of that minority in this democratic society? Would it be the same position that a minority holds in any democracy?

In every democracy laws are decided by majority decision, and every citizen must obey them. However, it is one of the basic democratic principles that matters of individual conscience, of religious faith and private morality, are not subject to majority decision. The majority rules not over right or wrong, truth or falsehood, but only on matters directly affecting the public welfare. One might even say that in matters of right or wrong in the ethical sense, true or false in their epistemological significance, the majority is mostly wrong. The pathfinders in human history have always been individuals, minorities, who stood up to the majority.

A democratic society is essentially a political organization, dealing exclusively with affairs of a practical, utilitarian public concern. Therein lies its moral legitimation. The moment a society attempts to rule over the conscience of its members, determining their religious faith and dictating their personal value system, it becomes immoral, and it ceases to be a democracy. But the Torah does require faith; it does involve the private conscience; it does present the Jew with an entire system of values, with a complete way of life to be followed. Halacha may well function in a democratic society on one condition: that all its members freely and unanimously accept the authority of the

Torah. The moment a dissident minority emerged upon whom the discipline of the halacha would have to be imposed by the will of the majority, its democratic structure would be shattered. For a society to function democratically yet in accordance with halacha, it would have to be continuously unanimous regarding its acceptance of halacha. This, of course, is utopia; maybe "at the end of days," in the time of the Messiah.

One might say that in the present conditions the community of an Orthodox yeshiva is a halachic society that functions fully democratically. One enters it and belongs to it in complete personal freedom and responsibility. The same might be said about an Orthodox community like New Square in the United States or the Me'a She'arim quarter in Jerusalem. But is this the kind of society intended by the Torah? The purpose of halacha is to guide the life of a nation, not just that of a sect or of a sectional community. Obviously, in the present phase of history and civilization, a democratic, halachic society of national dimensions is infeasible. This fact has to be acknowledged in all honesty. The responses to it may vary. Since halachic Judaism is not now nationally realizable, some may withdraw into the ghetto-like seclusion of the communal reserve. This approach reflects intellectual honesty and ideological consistency, two qualities lacking among those in the State of Israel, for instance, who wish to find their place within the democratic system but would by political means impose adherence to halacha upon it. A democratic society in our phase of history is by its nature a secular society, and the laws enacted by it, no matter whence they originate, are secular laws.

While a democratic society today cannot also be a halachic society, this does not mean that halacha cannot function effectively in a democratic society within a national framework. But it should be understood that nothing achieved by political punch is helpful. Not only does the authority method not work, but it is counterproductive. It engenders resentment and hostility. Halacha belongs in the realm of the spirit, and in the spiritual realm nothing fails like compulsion.

The method that teachers and followers of halachic Judaism have to adopt today is that of persuasion. The task is twofold. First, one has to interpret the teaching and its meaning for the searching, questioning, doubting contemporary Jew. This has to be done from the classical sources of Judaism and its halacha. The task requires talmudic scholars of a high order. But scholarship is not enough. The scholar has to be familiar with the spirit of the times, understanding its intellectual and emotional preoccupations. Only thus can he meet the challenge of each new day. Second, one has to restore halacha to its original function. In struggling with the problems of the day, halacha must once again reveal itself as the wisdom of the feasible, giving priority to the ethical. This requires that teachers of halacha accept personal responsibility for their decisions, as demanded in the Talmud itself. They ought to do so by following the advice of R. Abraham the son of Maimonides, freeing themselves of all Karaite inclinations and treating the principles and cases of the Oral Torah only as examples, deriving therefrom the ability to rule in each new case "as the judge sees it with his own eyes."

Not only does the method of authority not work, it actually defeats the eternal validity of the Torah. The Torah is eternal because it has a word, a teaching, for each generation. Every day the Torah should seem as new to you as if it had been given that day, says the Midrash. One can find the word that has been waiting for this hour to be revealed only if he faces the challenge of each new situation in the history of the generations of Israel and attempts to deal with it in intellectual and ethical honesty. Alas, those authorized to impose laws of the Torah do not care to understand the nature of the confrontation with the *zeitgeist*. They take the easy way out. They do not search for the word intended for this hour, for this generation. If they have the authority, they impose the teaching meant for yesterday, and thus they miss hearing the word that the eternal Torah was planning for today, for this generation, for this new moment in the history of the Jewish people.

Notes

CHAPTER ONE

1. For example, Baba Kama 46b.

2. Baba Metzia 47b; and the commentary of *Nimukei Yosef* on the relevant passage, which appears at 28b in the commentary of R. Isaac Alfasi (Rif).

3. Ketubot 22a.

4. Sanhedrin 74a.

5. By formal betrothal I am referring to *erusin*, the halachic form of marriage, which, however, does not allow husband and wife to actually live together until *nisuin*, the ceremony, usually under a *hupa*, a marriage canopy.

6. Deuteronomy 24:4.

7. Yevamot 11b; Tosafot ad loc., s.v. *lerabot sota*.

8. The *aguna*, or "anchored" woman, is one whose husband is missing or estranged without having divorced her. Because she is not divorced, and there is no proof of his death, she continues to be legally married to him and therefore unable to remarry.

9. Ketubot 2b–3a.

10. Cf. Brachot 37a; Yevamot 108a; Gitin 15a; Ketubot 48b; Kidushin 59b.

11. Gitin 67a.

12. Shabbat 60b.

13. Brachot 23b.

14. Mishna Eduyot 1:5; Ra'avad's commentary ad loc.; cf. Maimonides' comments there as well. Cf. Eliezer Berkovits, *Halacha: Its*

Authority and Function (Jerusalem: Mosad Harav Kook, 2006), pp. 28–29 [Hebrew].

15. Deuteronomy 21:10–14.
16. Kidushin 21b.
17. Bechorot 13a.
18. *"Heicha de'efshar efshar; heicha delo efshar lo efshar."* Hulin 11b.
19. Gitin 28a.
20. Yevamot 36b–37a.
21. Rosh Hashana 23b.
22. Avoda Zara 36a.
23. Beitza 36b; Baba Batra 60b; Tosafot ad loc.
24. Sanhedrin 11a.
25. Suka 26a.
26. Yoma 73b.
27. Deuteronomy 15:9.
28. Mishna Shvi'it 10:3; Gitin 36a–b.
29. Yevamot 16a.
30. Sanhedrin 12a.
31. Sanhedrin 26a.
32. Shevuot 45a.
33. Mishna Gitin 5:3.
34. Mishna Baba Kama 10:3.
35. Rashi's commentary on Baba Kama 115a.
36. Baba Batra 175b.
37. Hulin 49b, 76b, 77a.
38. Bechorot 40a.
39. Pesahim 20b, 55b; Shabbat 154b; Baba Kama 117a; Baba Metzia 38a–b.
40. *Sifrei*, Re'eh 16:13.
41. Leviticus 12:6, 8.
42. Kritot 8a.
43. The reference is to Psalms 119:126, "It is time for the Eternal to work; they have violated your law," to which the rabbis gave the following midrashic interpretation: "At times one has to work for God by voiding his law." For the discussion of this principle, see pp. 97-106.
44. Maimonides, *Mishneh Torah*, Laws of Those Requiring Atoning Sacrifices 1:10. See also his commentary on the Mishna, Kritot 8a.

45. Deuteronomy 6:18.

46. Proverbs 3:17.

47. Proverbs 2:20.

48. Gitin 59b.

49. Suka 32b.

50. Shabbat 63a.

51. The *kal vahomer*, a conclusion from a minor to a major.

52. Yevamot 87b.

53. Baba Kama 82b–83a.

54. Exodus 21:29.

55. Sanhedrin 15b.

56. Deuteronomy 25:3.

57. Makot 22a–23a; Sanhedrin 10a.

58. Brachot 20a.

59. For the sources, see Brachot 19b–20a; Jerusalem Kila'im 9:1; Jerusalem Brachot 3:1.

60. Hagiga 3:7.

61. Hagiga 26a.

62. Moed Katan 27b.

63. Ta'anit 26b, 31f.

64. Baba Metzia 10a.

65. Kidushin 63a.

66. Gitin 59a–b; *Tosefta* ad loc., 3:18.

67. This is not the only limitation on the law for this reason. See Baba Metzia 30b, 24b; Baba Kama 99b; Ketubot 97a.

68. Baba Metzia 108a, 35a.

69. Deuteronomy 6:17–18.

70. Baba Metzia 83a; for the biblical quotation, see Proverbs 2:20.

71. Jerusalem Gitin 6:6. Usually, the stories in both the Babylonian and Jerusalem Talmuds are confused with regard to what is known as *lifnim mishurat hadin*.

72. Deuteronomy 23:3.

73. Ecclesiastes 4:1.

74. Zechariah 4:2; Leviticus Rabba 32:8.

75. Kidushin 72b.

76. Kidushin 71a.

77. Deuteronomy 21:18–20; see Rashi's commentary there. For a more thorough discussion of the subject, see Berkovits, *Halacha: Its Authority and Function*.

78. Sanhedrin 71a.

79. Deuteronomy 13:17.

80. Sanhedrin 71a.

81. Makot 7a.

82. Leviticus 19:18.

83. Kidushin 41a.

84. Kidushin 41a.

85. Maimonides, *Mishneh Torah*, Laws of Personal Status 12.

86. Ketubot 111a, 56b.

87. Yevamot 112b.

88. Mishna Ketubot 7:10.

89. Maimonides, *Mishneh Torah*, Laws of Divorce 2:20.

90. Maimonides, *Mishneh Torah*, Laws of Divorce 2:20.

91. R. Joseph Karo, *Shulhan Aruch, Even Ha'ezer* 77:1.

92. Maimonides, *Mishneh Torah*, Laws of Personal Status 14:8.

93. For instance, the views of Tosafot on Ketubot 83b; commentary of R. Solomon Aderet (Rashba) on Ketubot ad loc.; the opinion of R. Asher ben Yehiel (Rosh), quoted in R. Jacob ben Asher, *Arba'a Turim, Even Ha'ezer* 154; also his Responsa 53:6.

94. Proverbs 14:10; "the rabbi," as quoted by R. Isaiah of Trani (Rid), *Tosefot Rid*, Ketubot 64a.

95. For the entire discussion, see R. Isaak Alfasi (Rif) on Ketubot 63a-b; Rashba ad loc., and his Responsa 1:192; Responsa of the Rosh 43:8; *Hama'or Hagadol* and Nahmanides' *Milhamot Hashem* on Alfasi ad loc.

96. Karo, *Shulhan Aruch, Even Ha'ezer* 154:2.

97. Responsa of R. Samson ben Tzadok (*Tashbatz*) 2:8.

98. Ketubot 77a.

99. Yevamot 106a, 44a.

100. Rosh, Responsa 52:6.

101. *Tashbatz* 2:180.

102. Gitin 3a.

103. Gitin 19b.

104. Yevamot 87b–88a. The legal basis for the non-application of the biblical law on testimony is discussed in chapter 2.

105. Gitin 33a.

106. Ketubot 2b–3a.

107. Yevamot 110a; Rashi ad loc.

108. Rosh, Responsa 42:1.

CHAPTER TWO

1. Baba Metzia 59b.

2. Cf. the discussion in chapter 1 about what happens when a majority is confronted by an individual whose opinion is acknowledged to be intellectually superior.

3. Mishna Rosh Hashana 2:9.

4. Baba Metzia 54b.

5. Mishna Rosh Hashana 2:9.

6. See chapter 1.

7. Maimonides, *Mishneh Torah*, Laws of Rebels 3:8.

8. Hagiga 3b; see Ecclesiastes 12:11.

9. Psalms 29:4; Exodus Rabba 5:9; cf. also Song of Songs Rabba 6:3.

10. Eruvin 13b.

11. Jerusalem Sanhedrin 4:2; cf. *P'nei Moshe* ad loc.

12. Quoted by Ritva on Eruvin 13b. Mention is made of the fact that this is "correct; however, there is also a mystical meaning, but it is not for us to delve into what is hidden from us."

13. See Rashi on Ketubot 57a, s.v. *mai kamashma lan.*

14. Sanhedrin 6b; for the biblical quotation, see II Chronicles 19:6.

15. Nida 20b.

16. Baba Batra 130b–131a.

17. See their commentaries on Baba Batra 130b–131a.

18. As quoted in Menahem Elon, *Hamishpat Ha'ivri* (Jerusalem: Magnes, 1988), vol. i, p. 345 [Hebrew].

19. See, e.g., Gitin 36b, etc.

20. A thorough discussion of the subject is found in my halachic work *Halacha: Its Authority and Function*, in the section "The Words of a Fellow Court," pp. 224-268.

21. I learned this interpretation many years ago from an old rabbi of a former generation. He told me that they had asked Rabbi Reines, the founder of the Mizrahi religious Zionist movement, how he planned to establish a modern Jewish state according to the Torah—how would he deal with the entirely new situation and its problems when, according to the halacha, one cannot overrule the decisions of a fellow court greater in wisdom or size. Surely, the present-day halachic authorities would not dare to claim superiority over the masters of the past. Rabbi Reines answered: "Pay careful attention to the exact formulation of the principle. It says, 'the words of a fellow court.' A court that functioned two hundred years ago is not my fellow scholars."

22. Maimonides, *Mishneh Torah*, Laws of Rebels 2:1; for the verse, see Deuteronomy 17.

23. Rosh Hashana 24b.

24. Responsa of R. Samson ben Tzadok (*Tashbatz*) 2:8.

25. Above, we discussed the subject from a different angle.

26. Yevamot 90b; Rashi ad loc.

27. Yevamot 90b.

28. Yevamot 87b.

29. See, e.g., Tosafot on Nazir 43b, s.v. *hai met mitzva*.

30. Maimonides, *Mishneh Torah*, Laws of Divorce 13:29.

31. Deuteronomy 19:15.

32. See our discussion above.

33. Ritva on Yevamot 87b.

34. One might, of course, ask, according to Ritva's explanation, what need there is for any leniency, because otherwise the woman might become an *aguna*. He acknowledges that this kind of testimony is as valid as that of the two witnesses required by the biblical text. His commentary attempts to answer the question, in our opinion with very little success.

35. Yevamot 88a, s.v. *mitoch homer*.

36. Yevamot 89b.

37. Yevamot 89b.

38. Cf. their commentaries on Yevamot 110a and Baba Batra 48b.

39. Baba Batra 48b, s.v. *tinach*.

40. See there, Gitin 4:2.

41. See I Kings 18.

42. Yevamot 90a.

43. Psalms 119:126.

44. Yoma 49a.

45. Brachot 54a and Rashi ad loc.; for the verse quoted, see Ruth 2.

46. See Rashi on Yoma 49a.

47. Temura 14b; Gitin 60a.

48. For the story, see I Samuel 6:14; for the discussion, see Avoda Zara 24b.

49. Ezra 8:35; Temura 15.

50. Nehemiah 8:4; Yoma 69b.

51. Menahot 96a–b.

CHAPTER THREE

1. R. Joseph Albo *Sefer Ha'ikarim* 3:23.

2. Deuteronomy 6:18; regarding the halachic significance of this verse, see the discussion in chapter 1, "The Priority of the Ethical."

3. Nahmanides on Deuteronomy 6:18.

4. Leviticus 19:6.

5. Cf. Maggid Mishneh on Maimonides, *Mishneh Torah*, Laws of Neighbors 14:5.

6. See the discussion in chapter 2, "Not in Heaven."

7. See the discussion in chapter 1, "The Example of Marriage and Divorce Law."

8. See the discussion in chapter 2, "It Is Time to Act for God."

9. See the discussion in chapter 2, "Only What the Judge's Eyes See."

10. Rosh Hashana 25b.

11. I Samuel 12:11.

12. Psalms 99:6.

13. Deuteronomy 17:9.

14. Ecclesiastes 7:10.

15. See the discussion in chapter 1, "The Priority of the Ethical."

16. See the discussion in chapter 1, "The Wisdom of the Feasible."

17. Jeremiah 29:6.

18. Ketubot 52b.

19. See the discussion in chapter 2, "It Is Time to Act for God."

20. See the discussion in chapter 2, "'Uprooting' Biblical Commandments?"

21. See the discussion in chapter 1, "The Priority of the Ethical."

22. See the discussion in chapter 1, "The Wisdom of the Feasible."

23. Isaiah 54:13.

24. See the discussion in chapter 2, "'Uprooting' Biblical Commandments?"

25. Some of them are discussed in chapter 1, for instance, regarding "The Example of Marriage and Divorce Law."

26. See the discussion in chapter 1, "Common Sense."

27. See the discussion in chapter 1, "The Wisdom of the Feasible."

28. See the discussion in chapter 1, "The Priority of the Ethical."

29. See the discussion in chapter 1, "The Priority of the Ethical."

30. See the discussion in chapter 2, "These as Well as Those Are Words of the Living God."

31. See the discussion in chapter 2, "'Uprooting' Biblical Commandments?"

32. Exodus 34:27.

33. Cf. Immanuel Kant, *Grounding for the Metaphysics of Morals*, trans. James W. Ellington (Indianapolis: Hackett, 1981); the quotations are from Kant, *The Philosophy of Kant as Contained in Extracts from His Own Writings*, selected and translated by John Watson (1891).

34. For a more detailed discussion of this subject, see my *Crisis and Faith* (New York: Sanhedrin, 1976).

CHAPTER FOUR

1. See Genesis Rabba 16:7.

2. Temura 14b; Gitin 60b.

3. See the discussion in chapter 2, "It Is Time to Act for God."

4. Maimonides, *Mishneh Torah*, introduction.

5. See the discussion in chapter 1, "Common Sense."

6. Temura 14b.

7. Cf. Raavad's objection in his comments on Maimonides' introduction. For criticism of *Shulhan Aruch* as a code of law, see Menahem Elon, *Hamishpat Ha'ivri*, vol. 2, p. 1145, etc.

8. See the discussion in chapter 2, "Only What the Judge's Eyes See."

9. Maimonides, however, is of the opinion that the practice applies even to contemporary rabbinical courts. See his *Mishneh Torah*, Laws of Rebels 2:1, and the problems raised by the comments of *Kesef Mishneh* ad loc.

10. See the discussion in chapter 2, "Only What the Judge's Eyes See."

11. For a discussion of this subject and suggestions for method and curriculum, see my essay "A Contemporary Rabbinical School for Orthodox Jewry," *Tradition* 12:2 (Fall 1971), pp. 5–20.

12. See the discussion in chapter 2, "It Is Time to Act for God."

13. See the discussion in chapter 1, "Common Sense."

14. Sanhedrin 27a.

15. See the discussion in chapter 1, "The Example of Marriage and Divorce Law."

16. See the discussion in chapter 2, "Only What the Judge's Eyes See."

17. For an in-depth halachic discussion, see my essay "The Halacha Concerning Autopsies," *Sinai* 69:1–6, 1971, pp. 45–66 [Hebrew].

18. Leviticus 25:3.

19. Deuteronomy 15:1–2.

20. See the discussion in chapter 1, "The Wisdom of the Feasible."

21. Leviticus 25:20–21.

22. See Abraham Isaac Kook, *Shabbat Ha'aretz*, "*Hilchot Shvi'it*," introduction, par. 14.

23. See the discussion in chapter 1, "The Wisdom of the Feasible."

24. See the discussion in chapter 1, "The Wisdom of the Feasible." See also Sanhedrin 26a; cf. Maimonides, *Mishneh Torah*, Laws of the Sabbatical and Jubilee Years 1:11, and Radbaz ad loc.

25. See chapter 3.

26. See Jerusalem Demai 2:1.

27. See Numbers 21:4.

28. II Kings 18:4.

29. Hulin 6b.

30. Jerusalem Ta'anit 3:1.

31. Ibid.

32. Cf. also Rashi on Gitin 36a, s.v. *bashvi'it bazman hazeh*.

33. See *Sifrei*, Pinhas 133; Psalms 145:9.

34. See the discussion in chapter 1, "The Example of Marriage and Divorce Law."

35. Shabbat 56a.

36. See the discussion in chapter 1, "The Example of Marriage and Divorce Law."

37. R. Joseph Karo, *Shulhan Aruch, Even Ha'ezer*, Laws of Levirate Marriage 165.

38. Deuteronomy 25:5–9.

39. See, for instance, the Responsa of R. Samson ben Tzadok (*Tashbatz*) 2:8.

40. Years later Rabbi Leo Jung of New York approached Rabbi Weinberg, who then lived in Montreux, Switzerland, to propose a solution to the manifold *aguna* problem. In those days Rabbi Weinberg's health had been greatly weakened by his concentration-camp experiences. He advised Rabbi Jung to ask me to work on the problem. (I assume the memory of our joint Berlin experience induced him to do so.) In response to this appeal of my revered teacher, I wrote my halachic work *Conditionality in Marriage and Divorce* (Jerusalem: Mosad Harav Kook, 2008) [Hebrew].

41. See Joseph Karo, *Shulhan Aruch, Hoshen Hamishpat* 34:4; *Me'irat Einayim* ad loc. 6, quoting *Mordechai*; Responsa of Rivash 314.

42. See my article "Conversion 'According to Halacha': What Is It?" *Judaism* 23:4 (Fall 1974); and my book *Crisis and Faith*.

43. Yevamot 24b.

44. Shabbat 31a; Tosafot ad loc., s.v. *lo bimei*.

45. Menahot 44:9.

46. See R. Jacob ben Asher, *Arba'a Turim, Yoreh Deah* 268.

47. Sanhedrin 99.

48. Yevamot 47a.

49. Maimonides, *Mishneh Torah*, Laws of Forbidden Relationships 13:17.

50. See R. Jacob ben Asher, *Arba'a Turim, Yoreh Deah* 268:3, 42.

51. Kidushin 70a.

52. Gitin 88b.

53. Sanhedrin 7b.

54. See R. Isaac Alfasi (Rif) on Yevamot 45b.

55. Even civil marriages are recognized by numerous authorities as halachically valid and requiring a *get* for their dissolution. See, e.g., the discussion of the subject in *S'ridei Eish* 3:51. See also *Tzofnat Pa'aneah* 1:26 and *Melamed Leho'il,* 3:20.

Chapter Five

1. Maimonides, *Mishneh Torah*, Laws of Sanhedrin 1:1.

2. See, e.g., the Responsa of Rivash.

3. Shabbat 88a.

4. Cf. the discussion in chapter 2, "Not in Heaven."

5. Maimonides, *Mishneh Torah*, Laws of Rebels 2:1.

6. See *Kesef Mishneh* on Maimonides, *Mishneh Torah*, Laws of Rebels 2:1.

7. See the discussion in chapter 4, "Halacha in Exile."

Index